MW01135482

# ALSO BY TIM ENGLISH

### Popology:
*The Music of the Era in the Lives of Four Icons of the 1960s : JFK, Martin Luther King, Robert Kennedy, and Thomas Merton*

### Sounds Like Teen Spirit:
*Stolen Melodies, Ripped-Off Riffs, and the Secret History of Rock and Roll*

# JOHN LENNON 1980 PLAYLIST

## TIM ENGLISH

# TABLE OF CONTENTS

# INTRODUCTION

JOHN LENNON. 1980. WE KNOW how this story ends, and it's still painful all these years later. Beyond the shock of John's violent death, for fans the bizarre thing was that he was taken away just after resuming his career after five and a half years. Lost in the horror of his assassination was the fact that 1980 was the year of John's creative rebirth. A return, not just to the recording studio for the first time in five long years, but also his revitalization as the unique creative force the world had come to know during the 1960s.

The inspiration for this rebirth was the same early rock and roll music that had galvanized John and changed his life as a teenager. In 1980 John would repeatedly express how he felt reconnected to the person he was before he was a famous rock star, or even a Beatle.

Way back in 1961, as the Beatles stood alone atop the Merseyside music scene, Cavern Club deejay Bob Wooler wrote perceptively in trying to explain the group's extraordinary popularity:

> "I think the Beatles are No. 1 because they resurrected
> original style rock 'n roll music, the origins of which are
> to be found in American black singers. They hit the scene
> when it had been emasculated by figures like Cliff Richard
> and sounds like those electronic wonders The Shadows and
> their many imitators. Gone was the drive that inflamed the
> emotions.... The Beatles, therefore, exploded on a jaded
> scene."[1]

So in 1980, John returned to the music of his youth to inspire him once again as he entered middle age, even nicknaming himself "Elvis Orbison" during the **Double Fantasy** sessions. He also listened to the popular new styles of 1980: reggae, punk or new wave, dance, funk,

---

1    Mark Lewisohn, *Tune In: The Beatles All These Years Vol. 1* (New York: Crown Archetype, 2013)

country, and even rap. In John *Lennon:1980 Playlist,* we'll take a trip through the year with John and share his listening experiences. We'll see how the songs he listened to connected with his earlier work and also sometimes inspired him to write new songs. John's listening choices make clear that he had an incredible breadth of not only musical, but sonic curiosity. His inquisitiveness was undoubtedly a key component of his musical genius.

John would later admit his disappointment with the albums he'd released after 1971's **Imagine**. He'd come to see later albums like 1973's **Mind Games** and 1974's **Wall and Bridges** as workman-like efforts by an artist who has lost his inspiration. The fact that in late 1973 he came up with the idea of doing an oldies album to be produced by Phil Spector affirms the fact that John thought his creative well was running dry. He seems to have been seeking much-needed inspiration from rock's founding fathers. That project became the **Rock 'N' Roll** album and took well over a year and a half to complete. It would stand as John's last new recording on the market for nearly six years following its release in February 1975.

Although John had booked studio time to begin recording a new album of original material in April 1975, he postponed the project once Yoko became pregnant.

The convergence of his son Sean's birth on October 9, 1975, with the expiration of his Apple recording contract in January 1976 provided two powerful reasons for John to step back from his recording career. John explained his decision to walk away from the music business to *The New York Times* writer Robert Palmer in November 1980:

> "By 1975 I wasn't really enjoying what I was doing anyway. I
> was a machine that was supposed to produce so much creative

*something* and give it out periodically for approval or to justify my existence on earth. But I don't think I would have been able to just withdraw from the whole music business if it hadn't been for Sean. I gave him five years, taking care of him while Yoko ran our business affairs..."[2]

These days, it's not unusual for major artists to have long gaps between releases, but in the late '70s it was unheard of. John's music had been part of people's lives for years and his absence seemed to puzzle observers more and more with each passing year. It's interesting to look at the output of John's contemporaries in the six years between **Walls and Bridges** and **Double Fantasy**. For instance:

**Bob Dylan:** Five albums of new material including the classic **Blood on the Tracks**, plus one double live album. Tours including the Rolling Thunder Revue in 1975-76, a World Tour in 1978, and tours behind his gospel albums **Slow Train Coming** and **Saved** in 1979 and 1980 respectively.

**Paul McCartney:** Four albums of new material with Wings (consisting mostly, though not exclusively, of McCartney originals); one triple live album, **Wings Over America**; one solo album, **McCartney II**; plus notable non-album singles "**Mull of Kintyre**" (a U.K. no.1, and to this day the biggest non-charity single in British history) and its B-side "Girls' School," "**Goodnight Tonight**," and its excellent B-side "**Daytime Nighttime Suffering**" with Wings, and "**Wonderful Christmastime**" solo.

---

2    Robert Palmer."John Lennon: Must an artist Self Destruct?" *The New York Times*, November 9, 1980

**The Rolling Stones**: Four albums[3] of new material including 1978's return to form *Some Girls,* plus the double live album *Love You Live.* U.S. Tours in 1975 and 1978; a European Tour in 1976; Toronto club dates in 1977; New Barbarians (Keith and Woody) offshoot tour in 1979.

**Elton John:** Six albums of new material, one of which was the double record *Blue Moves* (which might bump the total to seven); the live album *Here and There,* and the EP (extended play) *The Thom Bell Sessions.* U.S Tour in 1975; U.S. and U.K. tour in 1976; select British dates in 1977; a small handful of U.S. and U.K. dates in 1978; worldwide 125 show tour in 1979; U.S. and Far East tour in 1980.

**The Bee Gees:** Four albums of new material including the era-defining *Saturday Night Fever* soundtrack, plus a two-record live album. The Bee Gees had eight (!) U.S. no. 1 hits in 1975-79. Incredibly, they also wrote three U.S. no. 1 hits for their brother Andy: **"I Just Want to Be Your Everything," "(Love is) Thicker Than Water,"** and **"Shadow Dancing;"** one for Frankie Valli, **"Grease;"** and one for Yvonne Elliman, **"If I Can't Have You."**

**George Harrison:** Four albums of new material. No tours after his 1974 North America jaunt during which he infamously lost his voice, but memorable television appearances on *Saturday Night Live* in 1976 and in the brilliant Rutles "mockumentary" *All You Need is Cash* in 1977. John's 1980 demo of **"The Happy Rishikesh Song"** has music and lyrics reminiscent of George's infectious 1979 hit **"Blow Away."**

---

3    *It's Only Rock and Roll*came out in October 1974, just three weeks after *Walls and Bridges.*

JOHN LENNON : 1980 PLAYLIST

**Neil Young**: Seven albums of new material including one a one-off by the Stills-Young Band and *Hawks & Doves*, which was released just two weeks prior to ***Double Fantasy*** in November 1980; plus the two-record live album ***Live Rust***. Young recorded a lot of music during 1975-80 that went unreleased at the time including the 1976 sessions that turned up on the 2017 album *Hitchhiker*.

**David Bowie**: Six albums of new material including ***Young Americans*** which included John on "**Fame**" and the Beatles cover "**Across the Universe**," plus a two-record live album. Bowie was arguably the most influential recording artist of this era and someone who John greatly admired. Bowie did U.S. and European tours in 1976; and was sideman on Iggy Pop's U.S. tour in 1977 (John attended their New York concert, per Iggy); and a 1978 world tour. He also starred in the movie Nicholas Roeg's 1976 sci-fi movie *The Man Who Fell to Earth*.

**Billy Joel**: Four albums of new material. John was a fan.

**Bob Seger**: Four albums of new material plus a two-record live album.

**Paul Simon**: Not the most prolific of artists due to his perfectionist nature, Simon's late '70s production level is surprising similar to John's, so he's the outlier here. Simon released only two albums of new material in 1975-80, plus the 1977 single "**Slip Slidin' Away**," which was actually an outtake from his 1975 album ***Still Crazy After All These Years***. He also sang with James Taylor on Art Garfunkel's slowed down **cover** of Sam Cooke's **Wonderful World**, a no. 1 *Billboard* Adult Contemporary hit in 1978. Writer Lisa Robinson[4] recalled Simon play-

---

4    Lisa Robinson. *There Goes Gravity: A Life in Rock and Roll* (New York: Riverhead, 2014)

ing a copy of his new album—very likely *Still Crazy*—at the actor Peter Boyle's apartment for a group that included John and Yoko.

If we start counting in 1973, John and Simon both released only three albums of new material in those seven years. John hired Tony Levin—who plays bass on Simon's 1980 album *One-Trick Pony*—to play in the *Double Fantasy* band. In addition to appearing in the movie *One-Trick Pony*, Levin's added his distinctive fretwork to the hit single "**Late in the Evening**."

The point is that major rock artists of the era were expected to produce a new album at least every two years, if not annually. John recorded one album[5] of new material per year during his five years of activity from 1970 through 1974, plus several non-album singles including signature songs like "**Instant Karma**," "**Happy Xmas (War is Over)**," and "**Power to the People**." He also recorded the *Rock 'N' Roll* covers album. John's absence likely meant that he never recorded at least two or three (and possible as many as five) albums he otherwise would have released during those years.

Important artists that either released their debut albums or broke through in a big way in 1980 include John Cougar (Mellencamp), Christopher Cross, Michael Jackson, AC/DC, Pat Benatar, and Def Leppard.

The *Rolling Stone* Year in Music 1980 special double issue was on the stands in early December looking back on the preceding year. In his perceptive essay[6] Dave Marsh noted that the year saw the return of "lost legends" including John, Paul Simon, Bruce Springsteen, and Smokey Robinson. He also noted the rise of "underground" bands such

---

5    For convenience sake we'll count the two record *Some Time in New York City* as one album of new John songs.

6    Dave Marsh. "Hold On Hold Out," *Rolling Stone,* December 25, 1980.

as the B-52s, the Clash, and the Pretenders into the mainstream. The main theme of Marsh's take on where rock music stood in 1980 was a depressing one: marketing had produced a situation where "The unity rock once offered its fans now seems like a lie." He closes by noting that it's probable that "Rock has lost its ability move people in any significant way."

This was a bitter pill to swallow for many children of the 1960s who were now in or entering their 30s. It may seem a quaint concept today, but for many the hope that rock music could positively impact society died hard. This was exactly ten years since John had declared that "The dream is over" on *The Plastic Ono Band* song "**God**" at the outset of the decade, but for a lot of fans the '70s were a slow realization that he had been right. From a perspective of forty years it may come as a surprise to see how this theme of the 1960s as a golden era whose promise was still unfulfilled dominated John's and Yoko's interviews in 1980. John was continually barraged—to the level of absurdity—with the question of if and when the Beatles were going to get back together. It didn't matter if it was a fan on the street or a formal interview. Ten years since their break-up, the seismic cultural impact of the Beatles was only beginning to be grasped in 1980. But as John tried to emphasize, the Beatles weren't the point. The point was to open people up to the new possibilities that they could realize in their own lives. During the "Me Decade" of the 1970s many people, house-husband John included, were doing just that.

The musical world of early 1980 tempted John back into the recording studio due to his belief that the early rock and roll that he loved was again in fashion, and that artists like the B-52s and Lene Lovich were doing music inspired by Yoko's recordings from a decade earlier. By the end of 1980, John had released his first album of new, original material in six years, while also cutting an additional album's worth of new songs. His last days were spent working on Yoko's **"Walking on Thin Ice,"** a startlingly original song onto which John overdubbed an inventive guitar track only days before he died. This track gave the lie to critics of ***Double Fantasy*** who wrote John had gone soft. In addition, plans were reportedly afoot for a concert tour in 1981, something John had not undertaken since the Beatles last tour in 1966.

John was determined that ***Double Fantasy*** was to be a representation of where he was in 1980, a reasonably contented husband and father, older and wiser, and ready to share what he'd learned with the fans that followed him. He felt liberated by the fact that, at last, he no longer felt in competition with his earlier work.

Creative geniuses soak up the art and culture of their time, and the breadth of John's listening was impressive. From reggae to easy listening, punk rock to Bing Crosby, early rock and roll to ambient, jazz, blues, and gospel, John listened to it all and loved it all. From artists of his parents' era to artists that were half his age. An awareness of the new, appreciation of the old, and an extraordinary open-mindedness regarding sounds of all kinds. All of this is reflected in his musical journey during 1980.

For those of us that were there and those who weren't, lets take a moment to remember 1980, a world without fax machines, cell phones, the internet, texting, MTV, Facebook, Twitter, satellite radio and flat screen televisions. Many homes still had no cable television in 1980. While an estimated 16 million households were wired in the U.S., including the Lennon's, that number would quadruple it the next decade. Formats that are nearly outmoded today such as CDs and DVDs did not yet exist in 1980. If you wanted to listen to music you played a record, or 8-track or cassette tape, or you listened to the radio and hoped that a good song would come on. You had to put film in a camera if you wanted to take a photo. Public awareness of AIDS was still a year away. Listening to an FM radio broadcast from that time, one is struck by how slowly and quietly deejays speak. The mellow tones of the early FM years of the late 1960s are still there, soon to be replaced by a more frantic way of speaking as our pace of life has accelerated in the ensuing decades.

As John might say "It was so long ago..."

## NOTE:

Songs and albums that John is documented to have listened to are highlighted in **bold** text. Albums to which he listened to at least one song are also highlighted. In rare cases I have made assumptions that John would have been likely to have heard a song, and these are noted in the text. In most cases these are songs that would have been nearly impossible to have avoided hearing at the time, although there is no specific account of John listening to them.

# PROLOGUE
## 1977-1979

BECAUSE SO LITTLE IS KNOWN about John's life during his "house husband years," I'm starting our chronology in 1977-78 to give readers a sense of the music in his life during the run up to 1980. Accounts of John's life during these years are all over the map, but we do know that he was keeping up with what was going on in the world of music. Like his claim that he didn't pick up a guitar during these years, his claim that he only listened to Muzak or classical music during this time is a dubious one. It's probable that John—whose original plan was to stay home with Sean until he was five—knew during these years that he would return to making music in 1980, or shortly thereafter.

Disco was at its apogee in 1977, which was also the year of punk rock. John dug disco and in many ways was a godfather to the punk/new wave scene, which was a rebellion against the grandiosity and extravagance of much of rock music in the mid-1970s, and a return to the angry, stripped-down sounds of rock's early days. The American punk scene grew up around CBGB's and Max's Kansas City Clubs in the lower east side of Manhattan. John would later say that he followed Blondie from their early days around 1976. John's friend photographer Bob Gruen has said that he once introduced John to David Johansen, the singer of the New York Dolls, the forefathers of the punk scene in both New York and the U.K.

John and Yoko attended the January 1977 inauguration of President Jimmy Carter in January 1977. While many, including John, were no doubt happy Richard Nixon and his cohorts were out of power, the 1976 election would prove to be an aberration, as the Democrats wouldn't win the White House again for another sixteen years. The unfortunate but enduring legacy of Watergate would prove to be cynicism about government and its ability to help remedy problems. This was born out when both of Nixon's immediate successors—Ford in 1976 and Carter in

1980—were shown the door by voters.

It's noteworthy that the rise of Bruce Springsteen, starting with the **Born to Run** album in the summer of 1975 and the punk movement in the U.S. and U.K. in 1976 both took place in a vacuum created by John's departure from the music scene. As time progressed it was obvious that fans were seeking to inject music with a dose of the passion, anger, and energy that had fueled early rock and roll. The problem for John was that he wasn't twenty-one anymore, and he had no desire to "go back to high school" as he often put it. Never one for third person narratives in his songs, he wanted to make music that reflected state of mind as he approached middle age.

So he remained on the sidelines, but he was keeping an ear to the ground and no doubt thinking about coming back some day.

DEVO

"Uncontrollable Urge"

"(I Can't Get No) Satisfaction"

In a 2012 interview[7], Devo's Mark Mothersbaugh recalled a rather startling encounter:

> "One night we were playing at Max's (Kansas City) in New York City, and I was waiting for everyone to leave the club so I could go back in and pick up my gear. We were sitting in the van waiting and John Lennon and Ian Hunter from Mott the Hoople came staggering out and looked over. John Lennon saw it was me and stuck his head in the window. He was kind of drunk and put his face right against mine and went 'yeah, yeah, yeah, yeah, yeah' because he recognized it (Devo's song **'Uncontrollable Urge'**) as being an updating of '**She Loves You**.' That was one of my most exciting moments ever."

Mothersbaugh also said that John picked up on how the beginning of "**Uncontrollable Urge**" mimics "**I Want to Hold Your Hand**"'s opening chords. When the encounter was over he watched John and Ian stumbling off into the New York night together.

Late 1977 is smack in the middle of John's house husband years. There are few first-hand accounts of John's activities during that time,

---

7     "Made to Whip It Good," *The West Australian*, June 21, 2012,
      https://thewest.com.au/entertainment/music/made-to-whip-it-good-ng-ya-310626

but from Mothersbaugh's snapshot we can deduce that John was still a keen observer of the music scene, and he had not completely renounced the rock star lifestyle. Devo played at Max's Kansas City on many occasions during 1977, including shows in July and September, and multiple dates in November and December. At their November 15 show, their new fan David Bowie introduced them and also claimed that he would be producing their debut album that winter. That duty would eventually fall to Bowie's colleague Brian Eno, but Bowie did co-produce several songs for the record that came to be titled *Q: Are We Not Men? A: We Are Devo!*

It was probably one of these November or December shows that John attended, possibly upon Bowie's recommendation. In addition to "**Uncontrollable Urge**," the group's set list at the time included "**Jocko Homo**," "**Mongoloid**," the infectious "**Come Back Jonee**,"[8] and their inventive, nearly unrecognizable reconstruction of the Stones' "**(I Can't Get No) Satisfaction**," all of which would be included on their 1978 debut album *Q: Are We Not Men? A: We Are Devo!*

Devo's cover of "**(I Can't Get No) Satisfaction**" introduced the band to many listeners when it received widespread radio airplay in the U.S. during the summer of 1978. John had the song on his Dakota jukebox, according to Fred Seaman. Mothersbaugh later recalled that the band sought Mick Jagger's approval in a meeting before releasing the song. Fortunately, the head Stone dug it so much that he began dancing around his manager Peter Rudge's New York office and proclaimed "That's my favorite version of that song."[9]

---

8    The May 1979 issue of the *Trouser Press* new-wave music magazine featured John on the cover with the headline "Come Back Johnny," a reference to this Devo song. The article pleaded for John to return to making music.

9    High praise when you consider the killer version turned in by Otis Redding, which had a horn section playing the riff, as Keith Richards had originally envisioned.

Extolling the philosophy of "devolution," a sharp critique of American conformity and consumerism, Devo were out of the same Dadaist tradition that inspired Yoko's art. Devo's prediction that the basest aspects of our culture were beginning to dominate it was surely prescient, a fact that Devo's Mark Mothersbaugh pointed out in a *Vice* interview in 2018:

> "The devolution of humans (is) continuing. We were pessimistic, but not this pessimistic. We didn't think it was going to move this fast."[10]

Somewhat to their chagrin, Devo are best remembered today for their fall 1980 hit "**Whip It,**" which stayed on the U.S. charts for twenty-five weeks, peaking at no. 14 on November 15, 1980, just as John was watching his "**(Just Like) Starting Over**" ascend up the chart.

---

10    Andrea Dominick, "The Truth About Devo, America's Most Misunderstood Band," Vice, August 29, 2018, https://www.vice.com/en_us/article/43p97n/devo-mark-mothersbaugh-gerald-casale-anniversary-interview-2018

BLONDIE
"X Offender"
"Heart of Glass"
"Dreamin'"

In a postcard[11] to Ringo Starr sent in May 1979, John suggests Ringo record an old song in the style of a new song. The old song he mentions is the Les Paul and Mary Ford's 1951 hit "**How High the Moon.**" John recommends Ringo do the song with "female vocal harmonies." As for the style John suggests "disco-natch." Disco was all over U.S. radio in the spring of 1979, but rapidly approaching the point of oversaturation. John goes on to write that "Blondie's '**Heart of Glass**' is the type of stuff y'all should do. Great and simple."

As we shall see, John had the music of his youth and even his parents' era on his mind during the final years of his life. Therefore, the suggestion that Ringo cover a song that was then almost forty years old (having first been introduced by Benny Goodman in 1940) should come as no surprise. A young Lennon and McCartney aka The Nurk Twins performed Paul and Ford's song "**The World Is Waiting for the Sunrise**" during a one-off appearance as a duo at a Berkshire pub in April 1960.

Blondie might have been John's favorite group during the last years of his life. In his September 1979 taped diary, he mentions his fondness for Blondie's current hit, which was "**Dreaming,**" the first single from the band's fourth album, *Eat to the Beat*. "**Dreaming**" made it to no.

---

11    Hunter Davies, Editor. *The John Lennon Letters* (New York: Little, Brown & Co., 2012)

2 in the U.K. while it stalled out at no. 27 in the U.S. As a follower of the British charts, John would have been familiar with Blondie's song "**Sunday Girl**," which was no. 1 in the U.K. in May and June of 1979.

John's suggestion that Ringo record a disco song is surprising considering that Ringo had taken a stab at the genre on his 1977 album ***Ringo the 4th***, an album that was an unmitigated critical and commercial disaster (getting only as high as no. 162 on the *Billboard* album chart), and one that Ringo's career never quite recovered from. The album's failure resulted in Ringo being dropped by his label, Atlantic Records. And 1978's ***Bad Boy*** suffered a similar, if not a worse fate. Unlike earlier efforts, both albums contained no new songs written for Ringo by his erstwhile bandmates, including John. John's contributions to earlier Ringo albums included singing and playing on the new songs he'd contributed. These were "**I'm the Greatest**" on 1973's *Ringo*, the title track on 1974's ***Goodnight Vienna*** plus the hit (no. 6 U.S.) cover of the Platters' "**Only You**" (recorded at John's suggestion), and **"Cookin' (In the Kitchen of Love)"** on 1976's ***Ringo's Rotogravure***.

It should be noted that John's visit to Los Angeles in May 1976 to record **"Cookin' (In the Kitchen of Love)"** with Ringo at Cherokee Studios was the only time he set foot in a recording studio between early 1975's final ***Rock 'N' Roll*** sessions and the ***Double Fantasy*** sessions in the summer of 1980. This is a testament to his loyalty to Ringo. However **"Cookin' (In the Kitchen of Love)"** was hardly a top shelf Lennon composition and John found the session less than inspiring. ***Ringo's Rotogravure*** failed to match the success of Ringo's two previous efforts. John would later say that he never worried about Paul or George Harrison's ability to succeed commercially, but Ringo was another story.

John obviously cared about Ringo and the two were photographed at the Dakota on May 29, 1979, just a few weeks after the postcard was sent. Ringo would release no more new albums during John's lifetime, but he was recording what would become 1981's *Stop and Smell the Roses* in 1980. John planned to give Ringo the songs "**Nobody Told Me**" and "**Life Begins at Forty**," and he was also planning to record the songs with him in Los Angeles in early 1981.

Ringo and his wife Barbara Bach were visited by John and Yoko at the Plaza Hotel in New York on November 15, 1980, when the two old friends spent five hours together. It was here that John gave Ringo demo tapes of the songs he'd written for him.

---

## THE LITTLE RIVER BAND
"Reminiscing"

---

## FRANKIE MILLER
"Jealous Guy"

May Pang's 1983 book *Loving John: The Untold Story*[12] documents her relationship with John both before and after their "lost weekend" affair from 1973 to early 1975. It remains one of the few reliable first-person accounts of John the man. She provides a portrait that is often unflattering, describing John as someone who while being a caring, sensitive artist, was also violent and abusive, especially when he was drunk. Perhaps because he was used to people deferring to his needs, she found John was often blind to the needs of others close to him.

*Loving John* revealed that John and May's relationship didn't end with his reconciliation with Yoko, or even with the birth of Sean. May writes that they resumed seeing each other on the sly in January 1976 and continued to do so for the rest of 1976 and into 1977. These arrangements were always surreptitious and involved the cooperation of a third party who would provide a cover story.

May hadn't seen John in a year when he called her out of the blue during the first week of December 1978.

May writes that during their romantic reunion, John told May that

---

12    May Pang and Henry Edwards. *Loving John: The Untold Story* (New York: Warner Books, 1983)

there was a song that reminded him of "us." After John hummed a few bars, May identified the song as **"Reminiscing."** It turned out May had a copy of the song and she and John listened to it repeatedly—sometimes singing along—throughout the course of the long day.

**"Reminiscing"** didn't sound like anything else on the radio in late 1978. Befitting its nostalgic air, the music and harmonies recall the music of the big bands of the 1940s, an era for which John had a special, if surprising, fondness. **"Reminiscing"** makes reference to big band leader Glenn Miller in its lyric and John mentioned Miller in his 1980 *Newsweek* interview when questioned about a possible Beatles reunion and people yearning to return to "the good old days:"

"It's garbage you know – lets dig up Glenn Miller – I mean what the hell? He's on record! Glenn Miller exists on record!"[13]

Beatles producer George Martin would produce the Little River Band's 1981 album *Time Exposure*, which included the hit song "The Night Owls."

Among the songs May also played for John on this day were Franke Miller's cover of John's own **"Jealous Guy,"** which is on Miller's 1977 album ***Full House***. John was complimentary and observed that the Scot sounded like "a white Otis Redding." This is an accurate description and Miller's version of **"Jealous Guy"** takes the song in a new direction, giving it a soulful Stax-Volt style arrangement. It works beautifully and Miller's version surely surpasses Roxy Music's - which earned them their only U.K. no. 1 single when it was released in the wake of John's death in early 1981 - and maybe even John's original (sacrilege!).

Speaking of Roxy Music, John ran into Roxy singer Bryan Ferry at an airport departure lounge in Japan in 1978 and told him that he was a fan. Among the Roxy songs of which John was surely aware were **"Love**

---

13    Barbara Graustark, Vic Garbarini and Brian Cullman. *Strawberry Fields Forever: John Lennon Remembered* (New York: Delilah, 1980).

**is the Drug"** and **"Let's Stay Together,"** their cover of the Wilbert Harrison song; and **"Dance Away,"** a no. 2 U.K. hit in 1979. Drummer Andy Newmark was finishing a European tour with Roxy Music when he got the invitation to play on *Double Fantasy.*

May recalled that as the hour got late the two professed their love for each other, and John went home. This was the last time May ever saw John. May writes that John called her from Cape Town, South Africa, in June 1980, and that the pair talked for an hour and a half, with John promising that they would get together soon. Of course, that never happened.

TINA TURNER

"The Woman I'm Supposed to Be"

In a note from 1979, John asks Fred Seaman to get him a copy of the song "Supposed to Be." He guesses the artist who sings it is Lennon favorite Ann Peebles, but he is unsure and inserts a question mark next to her name. In fact, the song he's after is almost certainly Tina Turner's "**The Woman I'm Supposed to Be**," a track on her *Rough* album, which was released in September 1978. Although it was never released as a single, Tina performed "**The Woman I'm Supposed to Be**" along with several other songs from **Rough**, including her cover of Elton John's "**The Bitch Is Back**" on the Italian TV show *Luna Park* on April 21, 1979.[14]

*Rough* marked a key turning point in Tina's career. It was her third solo album, but the first not to have any participation from her ex-husband and musical mentor Ike Turner. Although it didn't catch on at the time, *Rough* did surround Tina with more contemporary producers and songs, a formula that would be the blueprint for her 1984 smash comeback album *Private Dancer*.

It's worth noting that Tina's career was at its nadir in 1979, especially in the U.S., so John was picking up on her music (even if he didn't know it) at a time when few others were. Her 1979 album *Love Explosion* also failed to kickstart her career. It would be a five year wait until *Private Dancer* did just that, selling an estimated 20 million copies worldwide. Appropriately enough, *Private Dancer* included Tina's cover versions of

---

14    Both performances are viewable on YouTube as of this writing.

John's "**Help**" and Ann Peebles' "**I Can't Stand the Rain.**" Funny how John made the connection between Ann, Tina, and himself five years earlier.

Eruption had a hit with their disco **version** of "**I Can't Stand the Rain**" in 1978. Their version was a no. 1 hit in several countries, but stalled at no. 18 on the U.S. *Billboard* chart.

"**The Woman I'm Supposed to Be**" was written by versatile Englishman Cliff Wade. Wade started his career making inventive Beatles-influenced psych-pop in the 1960s, the best of which can be heard on a cool compilation entitled *Looking for Shirley*.

Ann Peebles was indirectly involved in the two most infamous incidents of John's "lost weekend" in L.A. John attended her January 12, 1974, show at the Troubadour club where she was appearing with Al Wilson, whose song "**Show and Tell**" was a top 10 hit. This was the night John wore a Kotex pad on his head, and had a drunken run-in with a waitress who didn't find his antics—the effects of too many Brandy Alexanders—amusing. When John asked a waitress (sarcastically according to him) "Do you know who I *am*?" she famously responded: "Yes. You're some asshole with a Kotex on his head!"

A few weeks later John was bounced from the club for loudly heckling the Smothers Brothers. Earlier in the evening he'd been harmonizing with Harry Nilsson on (what else?) Peebles' hit song "**I Can't Stand the Rain**," which John once described as "The best song ever."

Peebles recorded for Hi Records on Memphis and was a protégé of Hi's founder, producer Willie Mitchell. Mitchell was at the peak of its success in early 1974 due to Al Green's string of hits. Note that John sings a bit of Green's "**Take Me to the River**" (possibly thinking of the Talking Heads 1978 **cover version**) on one of his 1980 Bermuda demo tapes.

Of course, John was a song-time fan of Memphis soul. The Beatles even had very tentative plans to record what would become **Revolver** at Stax Studios in Memphis. May Pang later wrote that one of John's favorite songs was Carla Thomas' 1962 hit **"I Can't Take It."** After her 1961 breakthrough "**Gee Whiz**," Thomas had hits with for Stax with "**B-A-B-Y**" in 1966 and **"Tramp,"** a duet with Otis Redding, in 1967. She is the daughter of Rufus Thomas, of "**Walking the Dog**" fame.

Moving south down Interstate 55 from Memphis to New Orleans, Ringo later recalled that John played Lee Dorsey's 1969 Allen Toussaint-penned song "**Everything I Do Gohn be Funky**" many times for he and Klaus Voormann while they were recording the **Plastic Ono Band** album in 1970.

BOB DYLAN

"Gotta Serve Somebody" and *Slow Train Coming*

This is one of three cases in this book wherein John composed a song directly in response to hearing another song. Perhaps we shouldn't be surprised that Dylan, Bob Marley (via Jean Watt's **Halleluiah Time**) and Paul McCartney (with "**Coming Up**" in 1980), were the only artists that could directly inspire John's creativity. John responded to Dylan's "**Gotta Serve Somebody**" with his scathing plea for personal empowerment, "**Serve Yourself.**" What seemed to infuriate John about "**Gotta Serve Somebody**" and Dylan's proselytizing album *Slow Train Coming* was Dylan's seeming to claim that his was the *only* way to enlightenment.

> "I don't want to say anything about a man who is searching or has found it. It is unfortunate when people say 'This is the only way.' That's the only thing I've got against anybody, if they are saying 'This is the only answer.' I don't want to hear about that. There isn't one answer to anything."[15]

*Slow Train Coming* was released in the U.S. on August 20, 1979. John began inveighing against "**Gotta Serve Somebody**" just two weeks after its release when he dictated his "audio diary" on September 5, 1979, sarcastically asking: "So he wants to be a waiter now?"

Sometime in 1978 John had taped two musical Dylan parodies.

---

15    David Sheff and G. Barry Golson, Editor, *The Playboy Interviews with John Lennon and Yoko Ono* (New York: Berkley Books, 1982)

"**Lord Take This Make-up Off of Me**" (released as "**Satire 1**" on *The John Lennon Anthology*) pokes fun at the face paint Dylan wore during the 1975-76 Rolling Thunder Tour—memorialized in the 1978 film *Renaldo and Clara*—to the tune of Dylan's 1973 hit "**Knockin' on Heaven's Door.**" Dylan's Rolling Thunder performance of "**Knockin' on Heaven's Door**" is included in *Renaldo and Clara* so it's likely John saw the film when it was released in January 1978. "**News of the Day**" (Released as "**Satire 2**" on *Anthology*) has John reading the newspaper while imitating Dylan's voice. Let's just say the joke wears thin pretty quickly. These recordings do provide ample evidence that Dylan was never too far from John's thoughts, even during the "house-husband" years. In an argumentative "open letter" to ex-wife Cynthia, dated November 15, 1976, and sent to *US Magazine*, John made reference to Dylan's *Blood on the Tracks* song "**Simple Twist of Fate**" while refuting claims his ex-wife had recently made about their marriage. The letter didn't see the light of day until 2017.

Dylan appeared on the second *Saturday Night Live* episode of the season on October 20, 1979, his first and to date, only, appearance on the show. He performed three *Slow Train* tracks: "**Gotta Serve Somebody,**" "**I Believe in You**," and "**When You Gonna Wake Up?**" John was home at the time, so there's a good chance he tuned in, although it's not documented.

Sometime in late 1979 or early 1980 John requested that aide Fred Seaman get him a copies of "Dylan's and Randy Newman's (*Born Again*) albums."[16] While this is probably referring to *Slow Train Coming* it's also possible the note is from 1980 and John may be asking for a copy of Dylan's second "Born Again" album *Saved*, a much less heralded effort that was released on June 23, 1980.

---

16    Davies

John reportedly watched Dylan perform **"Gotta Serve Somebody"** on the 1980 Grammy Awards telecast. The song won a Grammy for Best Rock Vocal Performance (Male) that night. **"Gotta Serve Somebody"** got to no. 24 on the U.S. Billboard singles chart. Over forty years later, it remains the last Dylan song to trouble the top U.S. Top 40.

Angry as **"Serve Yourself"** is, John was empathetic with Dylan's embrace of Christianity during his 1980 *Playboy* interview, stating that he understood the solace that religious beliefs can afford people, and speculating that challenges in Dylan's personal life might been behind Dylan's conversion. In the end **"Serve Yourself"** is not an attack on any religion but rather a polemic urging people take a hand in their own destiny. Although largely unbeknownst to his fans, John's relationship with Christianity was far more complex than his controversial comment about the Beatles being "more popular than Jesus," and the sentiments he'd expressed in **God**.

His ambivalence about spiritual matters was evident in a 1968 quote when John told an interviewer: "I've always suspected there was a God even when I thought I was an atheist."

John enjoyed watching televangelists on American TV. He had corresponded with Oral Roberts in 1972, sharing his admiration for Christ, but skepticism about organized Christianity. May Pang has claimed that John's only number one single "**Whatever Gets You Thru the Night**," was inspired by New York televangelist "Reverend Ike" Eikerenkoetter, who John heard use the phrase on one of his TV broadcasts. According to author Steve Turner,[17] John was so moved by the 1977 NBC television broadcast *Jesus of Nazareth* that he declared himself a Born-Again Christian, and even took Yoko and Sean to church the following Sunday. Sometime in 1980, John asked his aide Fred

---

17    Steve Turner, *The Gospel According to the Beatles*, (Westminster: John Knox, 2006)

Seaman to get him a Billy Graham biography.[18]

But the story that beats them all is the one told by John's long-time mate Pete Shotton[19] who described a 1968 meeting wherein John announced to his fellow Beatles and Apple staff that he was, in fact, Jesus Christ. Much to the bewilderment of those present, he wanted to discuss the best way of announcing this revelation to the world. Ringo broke the tension when he spoke up and said: "Right. Meeting adjourned. Let's go and have some lunch!"[20]

John's friend Elliot Mintz later said of him:

> "He did not describe himself as a religious guy and didn't go to church every Sunday but he believed in the Spirit. ... In many ways John was a Biblical scholar and could quote scripture at will."[21]

Originally slated to be recorded for **Double Fantasy**, "**Serve Yourself**" was only available on bootlegs and airings on *The Lost Lennon Tapes* radio series before finally seeing its official release in 1998 on *The John Lennon Anthology*. John recorded a version of "**Serve Yourself**" on November 14, 1980, on a tape generally believed to be his last home recording. The fact that he was still refining **Serve Yourself** at this late date may be evidence that he planned to record it for his follow-up to **Double Fantasy**. Had it been included on **Double Fantasy**, "**Serve Yourself**" would have gone a long way toward silencing the critics of the

---

18      Davies

19      Pete Shotton, *John Lennon in My Life* (New York: Henry Holt, 1987)

20      Tony Bramwell, *Magical Mystery Tours: My Life With the Beatles* (New York: Thomas Dunne, 2005)

21      The Editors of *Rolling Stone* and Christine Doudna Cott. *The Ballad of John and Yoko* (New York: Doubleday, 1982)

album who claimed that John had gone soft.

The last song on the November 14 tape was "**You Saved My Soul (With Your True Love),**" which also has a spiritual, if not a religious theme. In the song's lyric, John recalls that he "nearly fell for a TV preacher."

Dylan was a profound influence on John and the Beatles starting in 1964 when, during a weeks long engagement in Paris, they got a copy of *The Freewheelin' Bob Dylan* album and listened to it constantly. Among the "John" Beatle songs from 1964-65 that show a Dylan influence are "**I'm a Loser,**" "**You've Got to Hide Your Love Away**", and "**Norwegian Wood.**" Speculation had it that Dylan's *Blonde on Blonde* song "**Fourth Time Around**" was a sort of response to John's purloining his sound on the three aforementioned tracks, thus explaining the song's title. John had a copy of Dylan's 1965 single "**Positively 4th St**" on his Weybridge jukebox.

Dylan's three "Born Again" albums—*Slow Train Coming, Saved,* and *Shot of Love* have undergone something of a critical reappraisal in recent years. The era was the subject of a 2018 *Bootleg Series* nine-disc box set *Trouble No More,* and many critics and fans now agree that Dylan wrote and sang some of his most impassioned music during that time. Of course, Biblical themes played an important part in Dylan's songs both before (do "**Gates of Eden,**" "**Highway 61 Revisited,**" and "**All Along the Watchtower**" ring a bell?) and after his "Born Again" era.

Author Scott M. Marshall[22] writes that Dylan referenced Bible verse in his lyrics 89 times *before* his Christian era. As he had done in late 1967 with the release of *John Wesley Harding*—a spare, religious-themed album warning of worldly temptations that was released

---

22    Scott M. Marshall: *Bob Dylan: A Spiritual Life* (BP Books, 2017)

at the height of the psychedelic flower-power era—Dylan was now, once again, something of a contrarian party-pooper. This time he was propagating a stern self-righteous "get right with God" message into the cocaine fueled, hedonistic, pre-AIDS milieu that was 1979. Needless to say, a lot of listeners weren't eager be lectured about their lifestyle by one of their cherished rock icons, particularly one that hadn't exactly lived the life of a choir boy himself.

Dylan was not shy about preaching the gospel to fans at his live shows. Hecklers demanded that Dylan "rock and roll," and play his old hits, which he'd largely abandoned in favor of his new, religiously themed tunes. On May 15, 1980, Dylan answered a restless crowd at Pittsburgh's Stanley Theater in a lecture from the stage that combines elements of a Jimmy Swaggart sermon and standup comedy:

> "I know not too many people are going to tell you about Jesus.
> I know Jackson Browne's not gonna do it; he's **Running on
> Empty**. I know Bruce Springsteen's not gonna do it; 'cause he's
> **Born to Run** and he's still running. And Bob Seger's not gonna
> do it because he's running **Against the Wind**. Somebody's
> got to do it, somebody's go to tell you you're free. You're free
> because Jesus paid for ya!"[23]

Although he soon reconnected with his Jewish roots in the 1980s and in subsequent years, Dylan never renounced his "Born Again" era. It is best seen as an important time in the artist's continuing search for truth. It was also a time in which Dylan produced some great music, music that inspired another great artist.

---

23    Andy Greene,"Bob Dylan Planning Gospel Years Bootleg Series," *Rolling Stone,*
      October 20, 2016

NOTE: The *Slow Train* track **"Man Gave Names to All the Animals"** is considered by some fans to be among the worst compositions Dylan ever committed to paper. Therefore, it's surprising to find that the song was released as single in Europe where it was quite popular, even topping the charts in Spain for five weeks(!!) in early 1980.

DAVID BOWIE
*Lodger*

In a note[24] dated May 29, 1979, John asked Fred Seaman to get this new
Bowie album for him. Although it was recorded in Switzerland and New
York, *Lodger* is considered the last album in Bowie's "Berlin Trilogy," following 1977's *Low* and *Heroes*. Bowie and Iggy Pop famously decamped
to Berlin in 1976 in an attempt to escape the temptations of Los Angeles,
where both had been abusing drugs. Among the notable songs on *Lodger*
are "**DJ**," "**Boys Keep Swinging**," and "**Look Back in Anger**." Although
it sold only moderately by Bowie standards (reaching # 20 on the U.S.
*Billboard* album chart, while making the top ten in the U.K.) *Lodger's*
reputation has been enhanced considerably over the years to where it is
now considered to stand among his best work.

*Lodger* is a concept album about a homeless traveler. The album—
which had the working title *Planned Accidents*—was ahead of its time
with its incorporation of African rhythms (a direction further explored
by Bowie collaborator Brian Eno and Talking Head David Byrne's 1981
album *My Life in the Bush of Ghosts*) and Krautrock. Like the rest of
Bowie's "Berlin Trilogy," in can been seen as anticipating the music of the
1980s, and influencing the Brit Pop movement of the 1990s.

In the video for "**Boys Keep Swinging**." Bowie is seen dressed in
drag, portraying several female characters. Even for Bowie, this was cutting edge stuff, especially in 1979. John wasn't averse to dressing as a

---

24    Davies, *Letters*

woman himself, as he demonstrated by posing as a woman in photos taken in early 1979, in which Yoko dressed as a man. Perhaps the video contributed to the album's commercial difficulties in the U.S.?

In the spring of 1977 Iggy toured North America in support of *The Idiot*, his first solo album, with Bowie as a sideman, playing keyboards in his band. *The Idiot* was recorded at Berlin's Hansa Studios with Bowie producing, shortly before Bowie recorded his *Low* album there. Iggy Pop recently revealed that John told him that he'd attended Iggy's New York show in March of 1977. This would have been the show on March 18,1977, at The Palladium, for which Blondie was the opening act. Among the songs performed that night were three classics from Iggy and the Stooges 1973 Bowie-produced *Raw Power* album including "**Search and Destroy**," "**Gimme Danger**," and "**Raw Power**." The encore was *The Idiot* track "**China Girl**," which Bowie would successfully retool for his highly successful *Let's Dance* album in 1983.

At the end of their tour, Iggy and Bowie returned to Hansa to record Iggy's *Lust for Life* album. That record contains two of Iggy's best-known songs, "**The Passenger**" and the Iggy/Bowie co-write "**Lust for Life**."

Sometime during the summer of 1977, Bowie and John were photographed together while hanging out in Hong Kong. According to Bowie[25] this was not the only time he travelled with John during this period. Bowie later recalled that while in Hong Kong—with Sean safely back at the hotel with his nanny—the duo participated in typical rock star activities like getting "raving drunk" and visiting strip clubs.

Speaking years later about the "Berlin Trilogy" Bowie reflected:

"In some ways, sadly, they really captured, unlike anything else

---

25    Jones Dylan, *David Bowie: The Oral History* (New York: Three Rivers Press, 2018)

in that time, a sense of yearning for a future that we all knew would never come to pass. It is some of the best work that the three of us (he, Eno, and longtime producer Tony Visconti) have ever done. Nothing else sounded like those albums. Nothing else came close. If I never made another album, it really wouldn't matter now. My complete being is within those three. They are my DNA."[26]

As late as 2013 Bowie and producer Tony Visconti were talking about remixing *Lodger*, with both believing that the original mix of the album left something to be desired. Even so, Visconti described *Lodger* as "an important album for both of us."[27]

As we shall see, John's admiration for Bowie's work was also apparent 1980.

Along with **"Changes"** (sung in a duet with Alicia Keys) and **"Wild Is the Wind"** from *Station to Station*, *Lodger's* lead-off track **"Fantastic Voyage"** was one of three songs Bowie performed at what turned to be his final formal public performance, a benefit for the "Keep a Child Alive" charity at the Hammerstein Ballroom in New York on November 9, 2006. After never performing it live in the over twenty years since its release, Bowie exhumed **"Fantastic Voyage"** for his 2003-4 *Reality* tour, when its anti-war message resonated at the time of the Iraq War.

---

26    Ultimate Classic Rock website, "Revisiting Bowie's Berlin Trilogy," January 11, 2016.

27    Nicholas Pegg, *The Complete David Bowie,* (London: Titan Books, 2016)

## BING CROSBY

"Whispering"

"I'm Gonna Sit Right Down and Write Myself a Letter"

"Dream a Little Dream of Me"

If this connection seems incongruous, remember that David Bowie had just made a guest appearance on Crosby's Christmas special in 1977. The unlikely duo recorded "**Peace on Earth/Little Drummer Boy**" in London on September 11, 1977, as part of Crosby's annual televised special. Bowie had balked at recording "**Little Drummer Boy**" so the show's writers came up with the counter-melody "**Peace on Earth**" for Bowie to sing on the spot. Somehow the intriguing mix of generations and musical approaches works and the song has gone on to be a Christmas perennial in the four decades since it was recorded. Released as a single in 1982, the song went to no. 3 on the British singles chart. Interestingly John is mentioned in the short banter that Bowie and Crosby engage in prior to performing the song during the show. Pretending to be unaware of who Bing is, Bowie tells Bing that he likes older performers such as John and Harry Nilsson and Bing responds "You go back that far, do you?" Crosby died just five weeks later on October 14, 1977, after suffering a heart attack while golfing in Spain. Coming on the heels of Elvis' death on August 16, the world had lost two of its iconic musical stars in just two months' time, and John had lost two of the artists he most admired.

Elvis' influence on John and his musical contemporaries is widely known, but Bing Crosby's music touched John in profound ways, also. For instance, it was Bing's 1932 song **"Please"** (along with Roy Orbison's **"Only the Lonely"**) that inspired John to compose the song that gave the Beatles their breakthrough British single and jumpstarted Beatlemania, **"Please Please Me."** John was probably exposed to **"Please"** via his mother, Julia, singing it around the house. He described how he wrote **"Please Please Me"** in his interview with *Playboy*:

> "…And also I was always intrigued by the words '**Please**, lend your little ears to my pleas – a Bing Crosby song. I was always intrigued by the double use of the word 'please.' So it was a combination of Bing Crosby and Roy Orbison."[28]

Paul McCartney later revealed that the 1939 Crosby recording **"Girl of My Dreams"** was a special favorite of John's. It was among a handful of tunes that John's mom taught him to play on banjo during the years they spent time together when he was a teenager. For obvious reasons, the song apparently tapped into John's sentimental streak, which he occasionally gave voice to in his own work on songs such as the Beatles' **"Good Night"** and his 1980 composition **"Grow Old with Me."**

The Beatles eclectic pre-fame live repertoire included Crosby's 1936 hit **"Red Sails in the Sunset."** The Beatles version—sung by Paul—is preserved for posterity on the ***Live! at the Star Club*** album, recorded in December of 1962 during their last series of club gigs in Hamburg. It's a much faster and livelier affair than the Crosby recording and is likely based on the cover versions released by Ray Sharpe in 1959 (a B-side to his hit **"Linda Lu"**) and Emile Ford & the Checkmates in 1960. Both versions present the song in a rock and roll style that the

---

28    Sheff and Golson

Beatles' version closely imitates. Ford & the Checkmates scored a U.K. no. 1 with **"What Do You Want to Make Those Eyes at Me For?,"** which held the top spot for six weeks in 1959 into 1960. The Beatles crossed paths with Ford on November 24, 1961, when the Beatles played on a bill at the Tower Ballroom in New Brighton and Ford—a surprise guest—sang with Rory Storm and the Hurricanes, whose ranks included one Ringo Starr on drums. A photo likely taken that night shows Ford clowning with Paul and Pete Best.

John's love of Crosby's music lasted all his life. A Wurlitzer jukebox that played 78 RPM discs that Yoko gave to him at Christmas 1978 was quickly filled up with numerous Crosby 78s. Elliot Mintz was one of the few people to visit John and Yoko during the late 1970s and he later reported:

> "People kind of expected him to have rock 'n roll records in (the jukebox), but it was almost totally Crosby stuff. There were three songs which John played over and over. I still remember them. They were Crosby with a jazz quartet from the '50s, I think. He would banter and talk in the songs and John thought that was just the end. The songs were **Whispering, I'm Gonna Sit Right Down and Write Myself a Letter**, and **Dream a Little Dream of Me**. Yeah, those were the songs. I can still see John listening to them."[29]

If Mintz is correct about the origins of these songs, then they are from Crosby's 1957 LP ***Bing with a Beat***, which he recorded with Bob Scobey's Frisco Jazz Band, who provided Dixieland-style backing on several of the tracks. All three songs are standards from the big band era,

---

29    The Editors of Rolling Stone, Jonathan Cott and Christine Doudna Editors, *The Ballad of John and Yoko* (Garden City: Rolling Stone Press, 1982)

with **"Dream a Little Dream of Me"** being familiar to younger listeners thanks to "Mama" Cass Elliott's 1968 **cover version**. The song was part of the Beatles repertoire in the early days, with John singing lead. The Beatles played **"Whispering"** during a "Get Back" sessions jam in January 1969.[30]

Like many of us, John probably identified more with the music of his parents' era as middle age beckoned and he approached turning forty in 1980.

---

30  Sulpy

## DONNA SUMMER

*"Hot Stuff"*

Donna Summer's music was ubiquitous on U.S. radio during 1979, especially during the errrr ... summer. That summer would also mark the beginning of the end for disco, as exemplified by the "Disco Demolition Night" at Chicago's Comiskey Park on July 12 between games of a White Sox baseball double-header in which a huge pile of disco records was blown up. Whether this event (with undertones of racism and homophobia) compelled an anti-disco backlash or just showed that the genre had overstayed its welcome, many would later see it as a turning point for disco's popularity in the U.S. The economic hardships and long gas lines of the summer 1979 in the U.S. surely did not pair well with disco's "get down and boogie" ethos. Whatever the causes, the Bee Gees couldn't get arrested (at least as a group) after the summer of 1979, and "disco" was soon rebranded as "dance music." The following year would see Summer herself moving toward a rock-based sound that she first explored on "**Hot Stuff.**"

Andy Warhol ran into John, Yoko, and Yoko's mother at lunch in New York on June 16, 1979. "A guy next to us was down on the floor screaming, and finally he said 'Oh can I have your autograph?'"[31] This was John attempting to crack up the artist. Warhol dutifully noted the encounter in his diary: "John's very skinny now.[32] I don't know what kind

---

31    Pat Hackett, Editor. *The Andy Warhol Diaries* (New York: Warner Books, 1989)

32    Bitchy comments regarding people's weight and appearance occur frequently in Warhol's diary, so one shouldn't read too much into this comment about John.

of diet he's on, maybe rice." There are relatively few photos of John from 1978, but several pictures show him looking a bit bleary-eyed while visiting Warhol's office with Liza Minelli[33] in February of that year.

John was in Japan with his family from July 28 to August 28, 1979, a much shorter visit than the previous summer. Upon his return, he recorded his autobiographical audio diary entry on September 5.

Sometime around June, John wrote a note[34] asking his aide Fred Seaman to purchase Summer's "**Hot Stuff**" 45, the B-side was "**Journey to the Centre of Your Heart.**" With a more rock-oriented sound, "**Hot Stuff**" spearheaded Summer's dominance of the U.S. charts in the summer of 1979. After topping the chart on June 2, it was displaced at no. 1 by the Bee Gees "**Love You Inside Out**" before returning to no. 1 in mid-June for two more weeks.

"**Hot Stuff**" would prove to be the seventh most popular song in the U.S. for the year of 1979 according to *Billboard*. Next up "**Bad Girls**" went to no. 1 for five weeks staring on July 14, this in an era when such extended runs were far less common than they later became. A disco track, "**Bad Girls**" would prove to be the second most-popular song in the U.S. during 1979 per *Billboard*. Both songs were from Summer's two record *Bad Girls* album which was no. 1 on the *Billboard* chart for six weeks. The third single from *Bad Girls*, "**Dim All the Lights**," stalled at no. 2 in the fall, but Summer was at the top of the chart again in late November with her duet with Barbra Streisand "**No More Tears (Enough is Enough).**" Although it capped an incredible year, "**No More Tears**" would prove to be Summer's final no. 1 hit in the U.S.

John mentions Donna Summer in his *Playboy* interview as a contemporary artist that he admired. Summer ruled the U.S. charts in the

---

33    I wonder if she knew that John used to sing her mom's "**Over the Rainbow**" on stage during the Beatles' early days?

34    Davies, *Letters*

late 1970s. Among the songs John would have known are Summer's hits "**Love to Love You Baby**" (which would seemingly inspire Yoko's orgasmic sounds at the end of the *Double Fantasy* track "**Kiss, Kiss, Kiss**", "**I Feel Love**," "**Last Dance**," her disco-fied version of Jimmy Webb's "**MacArthur Park**," and "**On the Radio**," which was on the charts in the spring of 1980.

John had been a fan of disco for years. Asked by host Tom Snyder during his 1975 *Tomorrow Show* interview what he thought about the current music scene John said "I like the disco music which is out now … which is great. Great music." The year before he'd based "**Whatever Gets You Thru the Night**" around George McCrae's disco hit "**Rock Your Baby**" and had Shirley & Company's "**Shame Shame Shame**" on his home jukebox in 1975. It's interesting to note that the Rolling Stones were also fans of "**Shame Shame Shame**" and they recorded a still unreleased version of it in Munich in 1975.

We'll revisit Donna's impact on John as we move into 1980, including how he came to alter the title of his comeback single because of a song she had written.

THE KNACK

*Get the Knack*

"My Sharona"

*Double Fantasy* producer Jack Douglas later told Doug Fieger of The Knack that John was a "big fan" of the band's wildly successful first album *Get the Knack*.[35] The band's single from the album, "**My Sharona**," was a huge hit in the U.S., holding down the top spot in the *Billboard* "Hot 100" for six weeks from late August to early October 1979. As such, it was a ubiquitous presence on U.S. radio that summer, and would later be named by *Billboard* as the top U.S. single of 1979. Meanwhile *Get the Knack* **topped** the *Billboard* album charts for five weeks. Other popular tunes from the album were "**Good Girls Don't**" and "**That's What the Little Girls Do.**" It's worth noting that *Get the Knack* was produced by Mike Chapman, who was also behind the boards for Blondie's "**Heart of Glass**," a Lennon favorite.

The Knack wore their Beatles influences not only in their music—although Fieger claimed The Who and The Kinks were much stronger influences—but also in the album's cover photos, which seem to reference *A Hard Days Night*. They took their name from *The Knack ... and How to Get It,* the movie director Richard Lester made after *A Hard Day's Night*. They recorded for Capitol, the Beatles' label. Unfair accusations that they were comparing themselves favorably to the Beatles led to a backlash against the band (*Knuke the Knack*, anyone?) and the band

---

35   "Gary James Interview with Doug Fieger of the Knack," classicbands.com, http://www.classicbands.com/TheKnackInterview.html

soon faded into obscurity. The rock intelligentsia seemingly resented The Knack's success, which came at a time when more deserving bands like the Ramones were struggling to get airplay on U.S. radio. The Knack didn't help their own cause when they released a barely disguised "**My Sharona**" rewrite called "Baby Talks Dirty" as the first single from their second album ... *But the Little Girls Understand* in 1980.

Although John and his family spent much of the summer of 1979 in Japan, he was surely aware that the most successful band at the time was modeling the Beatles with their concise, melodic tunes, and even referencing his former band's image. In determining whether the time was right to finally end his sabbatical from the pop world, the success of The Knack would at very least have done nothing to dissuade him from returning.

It would take another decade of so before bands like Oasis not only weren't punished for their explicit Beatle homages, but were praised for them.

THE DOOBIE BROTHERS

*Minute by Minute*

"What a Fool Believes"

"Don't Stop to Watch the Wheels"

Sometime in 1979, John requested that Fred Seaman get him a copy of the Doobies' **Minute by Minute**. The album contains "**What a Fool Believes**," a song that was a no. 1 hit in the U.S. in April 1979, and ubiquitous presence on New York city radio. The song went on to win the Grammy Award for both Record of the Year and Song of the Year.

With the departure of lead singer and guitarist Tom Johnston, Michael McDonald was now the dominant force in the Doobie Brothers. McDonald and singer Kenny Loggins co-wrote "**What a Fool Believes**." Loggins was the first to release the song, which he included on his 1978 album *Nightwatch*, which was released six months before *Minute by Minute*. Loggins didn't release his version of "**What a Fool Believes**" as a single, opting instead to go with "**Whenever I Call You Friend**," a duet with Stevie Nicks of the then-massively popular Fleetwood Mac that hit no. 5 on the *Billboard* chart in the fall of 1978. Loggins and McDonald also teamed up to sing on Loggins' hit **This Is It,** a song they co-wrote which got to no. 11 in the *Billboard* Hot 100 in February 1980.

In addition to "**What a Fool Believes**," two other singles from *Minute by Minute* also made the U.S. Top 40: "**Minute by Minute**" (no. 14) and "**Dependin' on You**" (no. 25). Written by Michael McDonald and longtime guitarist Patrick Simmons, "**Dependin' on You**" is an interesting blend of the band's old and new styles.

Released on December 1, 1978, *Minute by Minute* was at the top of the *Billboard* charts for five weeks in early 1979. It's noteworthy that the last song on the first side of the *Minute by Minute* album is "**Don't Stop to Watch the Wheels.**" Written by Simmons, "**Don't Stop to Watch the Wheels**" is reflective of the Doobies classic early '70s sound, as opposed to the R&B direction the band had moved in since McDonald had come on board in 1976. Like John's "**Watching the Wheels,**" the Doobies' song contains the phrase "Watching the Wheels Go 'Round."

Might the Doobies' song have inspired John to write "**Watching the Wheels,**" a song that became not only a centerpiece of *Double Fantasy*, but also John's musical explanation of his five-year absence? It's certainly not a phrase one hears every day. Given the long gestation involved in the birth of "Watching the Wheels," it's possible. "**Watching the Wheels'**" origins lie in a song called "**Emotional Wreck**" which John began working on in 1977. After being retitled "**People,**" by 1979 the song had morphed into "**I'm Crazy,**" which is close to the familiar final version. It seems the piece didn't take on the name "**Watching the Wheels**" until 1979. Therefore, the 1979 timeline of John's hearing the Doobies "**Don't Start to Watch the Wheels**" means it may have inspired "**Watching the Wheels.**" Recall that there were numerous articles in the music press during those years questioning why John had left the scene and imploring him to return. "**Watching the Wheels**" was his musical response to those questions.

Asked to describe the wheels he was referring to in "**Watching the Wheels**" John stated:

> "The whole universe is a wheel, right? Wheels going round and round. They're my own wheels, mainly, but ... watching meself

is like watching everyone else. And I watch meself through my child too. ... The hardest part is facing yourself. ... It's easier to shout about '**Revolution**' and '**Power to the People**' than it is to look at yourself and try to find out what's real inside you and what isn't."[36]

John's interest in *Minute by Minute* was probably spurred by his wanting to examine what was popular at the time, but he might have dug the music, too. As we shall see, McDonald later lent his soulful vocals to another favorite of John's, Christopher Cross's "**Ride Like the Wind**."

On August 23, 1980, the Doobies released "**Real Love**," the first single from their upcoming album *One Step Closer*. John was working on his own "**Real Love**" song that summer, and had at one point planned to record it for *Double Fantasy*. Initial tracking sessions for the album had concluded by the time the Doobies "**Real Love**" was released, (although sessions were still taking place during late August) so it's unlikely, though not impossible, that the Doobies' song was a factor in John's decision not to record his "**Real Love**." The Doobies "**Real Love**" was a hit, rising to no. 5 on the U.S. Hot 100 that fall. McDonald left the band shortly thereafter and the Doobies wouldn't have another Top 40 hit until 1989's "The Doctor."

Proving again that imitation is the sincerest form of flattery, singer Robbie Dupree's "**What a Fool Believes**" sound-alike "**Steal Away**" went to no. 6 in Billboard's Hot 100 in the summer of 1980.

Starting in 1982, McDonald had gone on to a successful solo career. In 2020 he was voted into the Rock and Roll Hall of Fame along with the Doobie Brothers. Fun fact: McDonald co-wrote Van Halen's "I'll Wait."

---

36    Jonanthan Cott. *Days That I'll Remember: Spending time with John Lennon and Yoko Ono* (New York: Doubleday, 2013)

## THE ROCHES
*The Roches*

John asked his aide Fred Seaman to acquire this album[37] for him in the summer of 1979. The Roches—New Jersey sisters Maggie, Suzzy, and Terre—had built a buzz for themselves amongst critics in New York that year, and John was obviously eager to hear their music for himself. Perhaps the man that came up with the name Beatles for his band, was impressed that their name was a clever wordplay referencing an insect.

*The Roches* features spare, quirky, and funny songs that stood out in the musical landscape of the time. No one else sounded quite like The Roches in 1979. Fan favorites from the album include "**The Married Men**" (memorably performed by Phoebe Snow and Linda Ronstadt that May on *Saturday Night Live*) and "**Hammond Song**," the first track on the album. The Roches themselves were the musical guests on the November 17, 1979, episode of *SNL*, performing "**Bobby's Song**" (which was released on their 1980 LP *Nurds*) and Handel's "**Hallelujah Chorus**."

*The Roches* was produced by Robert Fripp of King Crimson—a seemingly incongruous choice given his prog-rock background—who also plays guitar on the album. A year later the bass player on the album, Tony Levin, was recruited to play on the *Double Fantasy* sessions. (Because of Levin's shaved head John dubbed him "Kojak," after the TV detective played by Telly Savalas.) *The Roches* was recorded in the autumn of 1978

---

37    Davies, *Letters*

at the Hit Factory on west 48th St. in New York, the same studio where John and Yoko would record **Double Fantasy** almost two years later.

Fripp would also produce the trio's 1982 album *Keep on Doing*. Suzzy Roche has a daughter with singer Loudon Wainwright III, singer-songwriter Lucy Wainwright Roche. Maggie Roche passed away in 2017.

Speaking of Loudon, he wrote and recorded a song about John's assassination titled "Not John." A largely matter-of-fact look at horrific event, the song manages to be both moving and disturbing at the same time. It appears on Loudon's 1985 album, *I'm Alright*. Loudon's son Rufus is friends with Sean Lennon and the pair duetted on an affecting version of John's "**Across the Universe**" at the *Come Together: A Night for John Lennon's Words and Music* tribute concert held in the aftermath of 9/11 at New York's Radio City Music Hall in October 2001.

## JAMES TAYLOR
"Day Tripper" and *Flag*

John wrote a note[38] asking that Fred Seaman get a copy of this Taylor's version of the Beatles "**Day Tripper**" from Atlantic Records upon its release in May 1979 as a track on Taylor's *Flag* album. John's request is a bit curious in light of the fact that Taylor didn't release "**Day Tripper**" as a single in the U.S. It's likely John got a copy of *Flag* instead since that was the only way to hear the song. Taylor's "**Day Tripper**" is an upbeat reworking, but the arrangement is missing the memorable guitar riff that dominates the Beatles' original.

*Flag* received a lukewarm reception from critics upon its release. For a single, Taylor chose to release his **cover** of Gerry Goffin-Carole King's 1962 Drifters hit "**Up on the Roof**," a song he'd performed live with King in the early '70s. His version of "**Up on the Roof**" got to no. 28 on the *Billboard* Hot 100. Although this marked the last time Taylor would crack the top 40 as a solo artist to date, his 1980 duet with J.D. Souther, "**Her Town Too**," made it to no. 11 in late 1980.

Taylor had a long history with John and the Beatles, dating back to his days with Apple Records in the late '60s. Taylor's signing was one of the few success stories of the label's "open door" policy with artists. His **self-titled first album**, produced by Peter Asher, was released on Apple in December 1968 and includes the now classic "**Carolina in My Mind**" (on which Paul plays bass and George sings) and "**Something in**

---

38   Davies, *Letters*

**the Way She Moves"** which would help inspire George's **"Something,"** John's favorite track on ***Abbey Road.***

Despite the fact that he'd been "discovered" by his bandmates and had recorded for Apple, John was lukewarm in his assessment of Taylor in his December 1970 *Rolling Stone* interview:

> "I'm not stuck on Sweet Baby (James Taylor)—I'm getting to like him more hearing him on the radio, but I was never struck by his stuff."[39]

John is referring to ***Sweet Baby James***, Taylor's 1970 breakthrough album that contained the no. 3 hit **"Fire and Rain,"** and the **title track.** Perhaps John was cross because the album was released on Warner Brothers label, not Apple.

In February 2020 Taylor gave a candid interview to *The Guardian*[40] headlined "I Was a Bad Influence on the Beatles" in which he discussed his early career and interactions with the Beatles during 1968. Taylor had picked up a heroin habit sometime earlier in the U.S., and the cheap price of the drug in London only made matters worse. Taylor was recording his album at Trident Studios in London at the same time the Beatles were sporadically using the studio, notably to record **"Hey Jude"** that summer. Asked if it was hard to kick his habit given the circles in which he was running then, Taylor responded:

> "Well I was bad influence to be around the Beatles at that time

39    Jann S. Wenner. *Lennon Remembers: The Full Rolling Stone Interviews from 1970* (New York: Verso, 2010)

40    Jenny Stevens, " I Was a Bad Influence on the Beatles," *The Guardian*, February 17, 2020, https://www.theguardian.com/music/2020/feb/17/james-taylor-i-was-a-bad-influence-on-the-beatles-lennon-love-and-a-life-in-song

too ... because I gave John opiates."

Asked if he was the one that had introduced John to the drug, Taylor responded that he didn't know.

John was certainly strung out during the Get Back sessions in early 1969, and for an unknown duration of time after that. The fact that Taylor and his then wife Carly Simon were friends with John and Yoko (the foursome attended a reception for choreographer Merce Cunningham in New York on January 18, 1977) only adds weight to his statements about John. Taylor's own drug habit would grow so bad that it famously alarmed even his hard-partying Martha's Vineyard neighbor, John Belushi.

Appropriately enough, Taylor was inducted into the Rock and Roll Hall of Fame in 2000 by one of the men for whom he auditioned in London to get on Apple Records back 1968, Paul McCartney.

**"Day Tripper"** received a more faithful cover by Cheap Trick the following year. But more about that later...

## RANDY NEWMAN
*Born Again*

***Born Again*** was released in August 1979, and John asked[41] Fred Seaman to get him a copy a short time later. John asked for this album along with one of Dylan's "born again" albums—likely ***Slow Train Coming*** but possibly 1980's ***Saved***—so it's possible John was expecting Newman to address religious themes on the album more than he does. Or maybe he was just a fan.

The ***Born Again*** album flopped in contrast to the success his 1977 album ***Little Criminals***, which featured "**Short People**,"[42] an improbable hit single. ***Born Again*** stalled at 41 on the *Billboard* album chart, and received a lot of negative reviews. The album's cover showed Newman seated at a desk wearing Kiss make-up, with dollar signs drawn around his eyes. In 2015 Newman claimed that ***Born Again*** was "the best record I've ever made." Newman's lyrics on ***Born Again*** were too caustic for some critics, for example "**Mr. Sheep**," in which Newman takes aim at a white-collar 9-to-5 worker, a rather obvious target.

Andy Newmark, who played drums on ***Born Again***, would be recruited by Jack Douglas for the ***Double Fantasy*** band. Newmark also played on George Harrison's self-titled album released in 1979. "**It's Money That I Love**" was an early critique of the "greed is good" ethic that would come to prominence by the mid-1980s.

---

41    Davies, *Letters*

42    Eagles Glenn Frey and Timothy B. Schmidt sing the middle eight on "**Short People.**"

*Rolling Stone* reviewed ***Born Again*** in tandem with the soundtrack of the Stephen Sondheim Broadway musical *Sweeney Todd*. Writer Stephen Holden called Newman and Sondheim two of the day's "finest song-writer-craftsmen (who) are both misanthropes intent on subverting the optimism generally associated with American popular music."[43]

Newman's songwriting differed than John's in that he often uses the "untrustworthy narrator" ironic voice in his lyrics, while John preferred first person narratives, usually inspired by events in his own life. However, both shared a biting satiric wit, and that is probably what drew John to Newman's work. The "born again" title refers to a religious awakening that evangelical Christians described. Then U.S. President Jimmy Carter claimed to have been "born again" and the term became well known during his successful 1976 campaign.

***Born Again*** features an ELO tribute of sorts titled "**The Story of a Rock and Roll Band**." In it, Newman name-checks ELO and their recent hit songs "**Mr. Blue Sky**," "**Telephone Line**," and "**Turn to Stone**" while performing the song in exactly the same style as ELO. might have done it.

In 2020 Newman wrote and recorded a song for the COVID-19 pandemic, "Stay Away."

---

43    Stephen Holden review, *Rolling Stone,* October 4, 1979.

M

"Pop Muzik"

In his September 1979 taped diary, John cited **"Pop Muzik"** as a current song that he enjoyed. John seems to have been familiar with Robin Scott aka M, and mentions him by name. Scott, who, by 1979, had been kicking around the British music scene for more than a decade, was the writer and producer of **"Pop Muzik.**" A very modern sounding, even revolutionary record for 1979, **"Pop Muzik** "became the no. 1 song on the U.S. *Billboard* chart in November of that year. Six months earlier the song had reached no. 2 on the British singles chart.

Speaking about **"Pop Muzik,**" Scott later reflected:

> "I was looking to make a fusion of various styles which somehow would summarize the last 25 years of pop music. … Electronic music was being employed for the first time in a commercial pop context. It had that quirky machine-like feel which was to set a trend for the next few years."[44]

Scott later claimed that among his inspirations for **"Pop Muzik"** was Donna Summer's pioneering electronic dance music hit **"I Feel Love"**[45]. In the ensuing decades, both songs have been cited as profoundly influential in the development of '80s pop.

---

44    Fred Bronson.*The Billboard Book of Number One Hits* (New York: Billboard, 1988)

45    Upon hearing **"I Feel Love** "for the first time, Brian Eno proclaimed **"I Feel Love"** to be "the sound of the future."

John likely enjoyed fanciful free-associations that Scott rattles off during the song.

Some of Yoko's **Double Fantasy** songs incorporated the electronic dance elements present in "**Pop Muzik**," including" **Give Me Something**," "**Kiss, Kiss, Kiss**," and "**Walking on Thin Ice**," a song that was recorded over a drum loop, and which proved to be John's final recording. John's last home recording tape from November 14, 1980, contains a brief snippet of a song idea called "**Pop Is the Name of the Game**" that may have been inspired by "**Pop Muzik**."

A remixed version of "**Pop Muzik**" was played at the beginning of U2's shows on their 1997-98 Pop Mart tour.

# WINTER

THE 1970S ENDED WITH THE Soviet Union sending troops into Afghanistan on December 24, 1979. The decade that started with the promise of detente between the world's two superpowers was ending with an inauspicious return to the darkest days of the Cold War. (In response, U.S. President Jimmy Carter began requiring 19-year-old males to sign up for a prospective reinstatement of the draft and led an international boycott of the 1980 Summer Olympic Games that were scheduled to be held in Moscow.) In even more calamitous news, that was also the week that Rupert Holmes' "**Escape (Pina Colada Song)**"[46]—which is regularly cited as being the worst song of all time—hit no. 1 on the U.S. Hot 100. Its two-week run at the top was preceded by Styx's even more insipid "**Babe.**" It was a less than inspiring way to end a decade that had given us so much great music.

But these were challenging times. The U.S. was in the throes of the Iranian Hostage Crisis, which began on November 4, 1979, when militants took fifty-two American hostages at the U.S. Embassy in Teheran. The crisis would drag on throughout 1980, dominating nightly news coverage in the United States like few stories had done before. In retrospect, our 24-hour news cycle can be traced to the Hostage Crisis, which gave birth to ABC's *Nightline* show that aired at 11:30 on weeknights and focused exclusively on the crisis during its early days. Though many critics scoffed at the concept at the time, CNN commenced operations on June 1, 1980, presenting news 24/7 for the first time.

President Carter's inability to get the hostages released (highlighted by a botched rescue attempt in May), was an important factor in voters denying him a second term in November. The hostage crisis fueled a long dormant patriotic fervor in the U.S., best exemplified musically in Charlie Daniels mid-year hit, "**In America.**" Daniels' song captured

---

46    Okay, I'll admit that Homes' top-10 follow-up hit, "**Him**," is a guilty pleasure.

the mood of many in the nation frustrated at the U.S.'s impotence in gaining the release of the hostages and angry that Carter hadn't struck back. Conservative Margaret Thatcher had become prime minister of the U.K. in May 1979, an office she would hold until November 1990, so a rightward political tilt was taking place on both sides of the Atlantic. A lifelong news junkie, John was no doubt following events closely.

The year got off to an ominous start Beatle-wise when Paul McCartney was arrested and at Tokyo's Narita Airport after unwisely stashing eight ounces of marijuana (that's quite a lot) in his luggage. Naturally, John followed the case with interest until Paul was finally released on January 25th. The arrest and cancellation of the Wings tour of Japan would serve as a death knell for the band that had seen so much success during the 1970s.

The first U.S. no. 1 of the new decade was KC and the Sunshine Band's "**Please Don't Go**," a ballad from one of the most renowned exponents of disco, and a signal that the genre's shelf life had expired. As his thoughts started to turn to possibly recording again, John must have been heartened to see that Smokey Robinson—one of his idols and inspirations—was back near the top of the charts after a long absence with his song "**Cruisin'**," which made it to the *Billboard* top 5 in February. Smokey's name came up later in the summer while John was recording "**Woman**" at the Hit Factory. After Yoko commented that he sounded like a Beatle, John replied "Actually I'm supposed to be Smokey Robinson at the moment, my dear, because The Beatles were always supposing that they were Smokey Robinson." The Beatles covered Smokey and The Miracles "**You've Really Got a Hold on Me**" for their second album *With the Beatles* in 1963. John later cited Smokey as the inspiration for composition of the Beatles' songs "**All I've Got to Do**," "**This Boy**," and "**Not a Second Time**". John had several Smokey and The Miracles songs on his mid-'60s jukebox: "**What's So Good About Goodbye**," "**I've Been Good to You**," "**The Tracks of My Tears**," and "**Shop Around**." Kim Karnes would have a hit with her cover of Smokey and The Miracles "**More Love**" in the summer of 1980.

Although he was ten years older, John likely looked upon Stevie Wonder as a contemporary. After all, a 12-year-old Stevie had the no. 1 song in the U.S. with "**Fingertips (Part 2)**" in the summer of 1963, half a year before the Beatles appeared on *The Ed Sullivan Show*. John had shared the stage with Stevie at the December 1971 John Sinclair benefit concert at Ann Arbor, Michigan and the One to One concerts in New York in August 1972. Stevie was also present at the infamous Lennon and McCartney reunion jam at the Record Plant in L.A. on the night of March 28, 1974, the first night of the *Pussy Cats* sessions that John was producing for Harry Nilsson. The ramshackle session is documented on the bootleg *A Toot and a Snore in '74* which opens with John asking Stevie "Want a snort Steve? It's going around." (The soporific *Toot* bootleg might be the best argument ever made against cocaine use.) John no doubt took notice that Stevie's "**Send One Your Love**" was at no. 4 in the *Billboard* singles charts that January. A beautiful song, "**Send One Your Love**" was one of a handful of non-instrumental taken from Stevie's ambitious movie soundtrack album *Journey Through the Secret Life of Plants*.

Motown had another huge hit with Michael's Jackson's "**Rock with You**." With 1979's *Off the Wall* album Jackson and producer Quincy Jones had perfected the sound and template that would soon make *Thriller* the largest selling album ever and elevate Jackson to global super-stardom. A song by Michael's older brother Jermaine would soon make a strong impression on John.

In his *Playboy* interview John complained that people kept trying to bring back the Beatles and the Kennedys, telling Playboy: "People want Ted Kennedy to be John Kennedy and people who used to be the Beatles to be the Beatles."[47]

In early 1980 the last surviving Kennedy brother, Edward, aka Ted, was attempting to recapture the White House, campaigning for the Democratic Party's nomination against incumbent president Jimmy Carter. The Iran Hostage Crisis helped derail Kennedy's campaign, as did a bumbling response when reporter Roger Mudd asked him why he was running. After losing several important early primaries, Kennedy staged a comeback later in the spring. Although he didn't have a realistic chance of winning more delegates than Carter, Kennedy continued his campaign against Carter all the way to the Democratic National Convention in New York in August.

After witnessing the almost nightly burning of the American flag on the streets of Tehran and the Soviet invasion of Afghanistan, Americans got some much-needed good news in February when the American Olympic hockey team, consisting of amateurs from the collegiate ranks, defeated the far more experienced Soviet hockey team at Lake Placid, New York, and went on to win the gold medal. Ronald Reagan would prove himself deft in sensing and exploiting the new patriotic mood in the country.

Rock fans could embrace Tom Petty and the Heartbreakers' album ***Damn the Torpedoes*** that winter. The album was produced by Jimmy Iovine, who was well known to John via his work as a studio hand on 1974's ***Walls and Bridges.*** John must have been attracted to the ***Damn the Torpedoes*** album cover on which Petty held a Rickenbacker guitar, just as he once had. ***Damn the Torpedoes*** would have been a U.S. no. 1 album but for the presence of Pink Floyd's ***The Wall,*** which prevented

47    Sheff and Golson

it. *Damn the Torpedoes* boasted two top 20 U.S. singles: "**Don't Do Me Like That**" and "**Refugee**." Iovine came to prominence as a producer with the Patti Smith album *Easter* in 1978 which contained the Springsteen/Smith co-write "**Because the Night**." One wonders what *Double Fantasy* would have sounded like if Iovine had produced it instead of Jack Douglas.

The Clash released their third album, the two-record *London Calling*, in the U.S. in January. The **title track** made reference to the March 1979 nuclear accident at the Three Mile Island reactor in Pennsylvania and declared that "phoney Beatlemania has bitten the dust." The preceding line was "don't look to us" so the Beatlemania reference was probably Joe Strummer's way of saying this was no time for nostalgia and don't look to rock stars to solve your problems for you. The *London Calling* song "**Spanish Bombs**" recalls the fight against Franco's fascist forces in the run-up to World War II.

It's worth noting that while both Joe Strummer and Tom Petty were huge fans of John's work, *London Calling* is a political album while *Damn the Torpedoes* is decidedly non-political. John would choose Petty's approach when it came time to record *Double Fantasy.*

*London Calling* was a no. 1 album in the U.K., but it made it to only no. 27 on the U.S. *Billboard* album chart. The "hidden" album track "**Train in Vain**" was widely played on U.S. radio and got to no. 27 on the Billboard Hot 100.

Very few photos of John had appeared in the past three years, so fans were intrigued when *Rolling Stone* finally published a recent photo of him in March. We see a heavily bearded John, nearly unrecognizable while wearing a straw hat as he walked the promenade in Palm Beach. His disappearance from public life had seemingly done little to reduce public interest in him.

In understanding where John and his interviewers were at in 1980, it's important to be aware of the pervasive air of 1960s nostalgia—of which the Beatles were a main focus—that gripped the U.S. from about 1974 onward. The '70s—which gave us a corrupt president, withdrawal from Vietnam, long gas lines, and recession—were no match for the idealized vision of the '60s that many people (even those too old to remember much of the decade) came to hold during the 1970s. It was against this backdrop that John and the other ex-Beatles were continually barraged with questions about when they were getting back together. John was wise enough to understand that you can only stick your hand in the river at the same point once, and that people clamoring for a Beatles reunion had missed the point of the whole thing in the first place.

QUEEN

"Crazy Little Thing Called Love"

"I started noticing what was happening when Queen did that Elvis sounding tune. I thought: 'This is my period again.'"[48] Queen's rockabilly Elvis tribute "**Crazy Little Thing Called Love**" was composed by lead singer Freddie Mercury on his guitar in just ten minutes. The first single release from the band's eighth album *The Game*, it was a departure from Queen's usual bombast and earned the band their first U.S. #1 single.

"**Crazy Little Thing Called Love**" rose to the top of the *Billboard* chart on February 23 and remained there for the next four weeks. It seems John took the popularity of the song as solid evidence that the rock and roll of his youth was now back in fashion. Thus, "**Crazy Little Thing Called Love**" marks an important turning point for John in the winter of 1980, as it compelled him to think seriously about entering the studio to record new music for the first time in over five years.

The first evidence we have of a fully realized *Double Fantasy* song is John's video of himself playing "**Dear Yoko**" at Cold Spring Harbor, Long Island, on April 11. "Dear Yoko" wears its Buddy Holly influences proudly, specifically the Texan's vocal on his 1958 hit "**Rave On.**"

It turns out that John had crossed paths with Queen—or their music anyway—several years earlier. Longtime Beatles aide Tony Barrow later wrote that John had turned thumbs down on his efforts

---

48    Robert Hilburn "John Lennon: He Doesn't Believe in Magic or Beatles," *The Los Angeles Times*. November16, 1980.

to sign Queen to Apple Records sometime around 1973. Upon hearing a tape that included what would become their first U.K. hit, "**Seven Seas of Rhye**," and an early version of their eventual worldwide breakthrough song, "**Killer Queen**," John pronounced the band's music to be "rubbish." Barrow gave up and Queen signed with EMI.[49]

"**Crazy Little Thing Called Love**" is one of several Elvis-influenced tracks to emerge in the wake Presley's death on August 16, 1977. Certainly, John was affected by Elvis' death, referring to it in 1980 as evidence of the dangers of having too many yes-men attending a star. "The king is always killed by his courtiers ... he is kept overfed, over indulged, over-drunk to keep him tied to his throne. ... That's what killed Presley."[50]

Among the other songs written for Presley were Bruce Springsteen's "**Fire**" (written a couple of months before Elvis died), which the Pointer Sisters took to #2 in the *Billboard* chart in early 1979, and Led Zeppelin's "**Hot Dog**," a rockabilly track on their 1979 ***In Through the Out Door*** album.

The R&B-influenced "**Another One Bites the Dust**" was the second song from ***The Game*** to top the U.S. *Billboard* chart, holding down the #1 spot for three weeks in October. That month also saw the release of John's single "**Starting Over**" on October 24.

Queen played John's "**Imagine**" in tribute to him at their Wembley Arena show in London on December 9, 1980.

Years later, Queen guitarist Brian May described John as "The coolest guy on earth," and wrote of him:

"...As time went on it was apparent that John Lennon was at

---

49    Tony Barrow. *Magical Mystery Tours: My Life With the Beatles* (New York: Thomas Dunne, 2006)

50    Graustark

the heart of this awesome power (that the Beatles possessed) …
It was the acerbic Lennon who kept The Beatles firmly out of
the trite, and into the extremes of dangerous creativity."

## THE PRETENDERS
"Brass in Pocket"

During his 1980 interviews John consistently brought up the Pretenders when asked about current music that he enjoyed.

In *Playboy* John used the Pretenders as an example of how he was more attracted to a particular song rather than an artist's entire output. "I can't say I enjoy the Pretenders, but I like their hit record." John was likely referring to "**Brass in Pocket**" here, but considering he was speaking in September, it's also possible he was referring to "**Talk of the Town**," a stand-alone single released by the group in April that got considerable airplay on New York City's WNEW-FM during the summer of 1980. Both "**Brass in Pocket**" and "**Talk of the Town**" feature James Honeyman-Scott's inventive guitar voicings.

"**Brass in Pocket**" hit no. 1 on the U.K. singles chart in January 1980, so it's likely John became aware of the song earlier in the year. It went to no. 14 on the U.S. *Billboard* Hot 100 in the spring. "**Brass in Pocket**" was written by Pretenders' lead singer and songwriter Chrissie Hynde and guitarist Honeyman-Scott. The song is notable for the distinctive guitar figure played throughout by Honeyman-Scott, and Hynde recently revealed that she wrote the song after taking a home a tape of Honeyman-Scott's playing the piece.[51]

Undoubtably one of the greatest debut albums in rock history, The Pretenders **self-titled** first album was no. 1 in the U.K. upon its release

---

51    Chrissie Hynde. *Reckless: My Life as a Pretender* (New York: Anchor Books, 2015)

in January 1980. With the notable exception of their cover of the Kinks' **"Stop Your Sobbing"** (the band's first U.K. hit), for which Nick Lowe was behind the glass, the album was produced by Chris Thomas. An old Apple hand, Thomas had served and the de facto producer of several of the Beatles *White Album* tracks in 1968 when George Martin was absent.

The Pretenders played not far from the Dakota at a Central Park concert on Saturday August 30, 1980. The previous Sunday they were the subject of a profile in the *New York Times* Arts and Leisure section, an article likely perused by John.

Women fronting rock bands was still relatively rare in 1980, so John likely appreciated what Hynde had achieved as the leader of the Pretenders. Taking strong exception to a question about why he was working with Yoko, John told *Playboy* that the era of male domination in pop music was ending:

> "They're gonna look back at the Beatles and the Stones and all those guys as relics. The days when those bands were all just men will be on the newsreels, you know. That's gonna be the joke in the future, not a couple singing together or living and working together.[52]

In her memoir, May Pang states that during her last phone conversation with John in June 1980, she told him she liked the Pretenders when John asked what music she was listening to. She writes that she told John to check them out and he said he would.

Honeyman-Scott was part of the "Rockestra" that backed Paul McCartney at the Concerts for the People of Kampuchea in London in

---

52    *Playboy*

December 1979, where the Pretenders also performed.

In a May 1980 *Rolling Stone* cover story[53] on the band, both Honeyman-Scott and Pretenders bassist Pete Farndon were surprisingly candid about their struggles with drugs. Sadly, men would soon fall victim to drug abuse, with Honeyman-Scott dying in June 1982, and Farndon the following year.

Honeyman-Scott influenced many young guitarists, most notably Johnny Marr of the Smiths—arguably the top U.K. band of the 1980s—whose fret work with the Smiths echoes Honeyman-Scott's jangly, melodic sound. Marr has stated that for years he played Honeyman-Scott's solo on the Pretenders' **"Kid"** to warm up before gigs.

In his October 10 interview with Robert Hilburn, John again enthused about the Pretenders:

> "I love the music of today. … It's the best period since the 1960s: the Pretenders, the B-52s, Madness…It's the perfect time for me to be coming back."[54]

Chrissie Hynde memorialized Honeyman-Scott with the touching "Back on the Chain Gang" in 1982.

---

53     Kurt Loder "The Pretenders Leather Love Songs" *Rolling Stone* May 29, 1980.

54     Hilburn, *LA Times*, November 16, 1980.

## CLIFF RICHARD

"We Don't Talk Anymore"

**"We Don't Talk Anymore"** got to no. 7 on the U.S. *Billboard* singles chart. In August and September of 1979 it spent four weeks at no. 1 in the U.K. The song was written by Alan Tarney, who also produced Leo Sayer's no. 2 hit **"More Than I Can Say"** later in the year. Tarney would go on to co-produce one of the iconic songs of the decade, a-ha's **"Take on Me,"** in 1985.

Tarney later revealed a mishap as Richard recorded **"We Don't Talk Anymore:"**

> "Cliff lost his place at the end. But he is such a brilliant improviser that he kept going. When he sings the bit about losing sleep and not counting sheep, he doesn't really know where he is."[55]

Before the Beatles came along Richard was the U.K.'s biggest rock star. John and Paul McCartney particularly liked Richard and the Drifters' 1959 song **"Living Doll,"** his first U.K. no. 1. Richard had a rare stateside hit in 1976 with **"Devil Woman,"** a 45 of which was on a jukebox that John was said to have owed during the 1970s.

Later in 1980 Richard had another U.S. hit with **"Suddenly,"** his duet with Olivia Newton-John from the movie *Xanadu*, the music from

---

[55]    Jon Kutner and Spencer Leigh. *100 U.K. Number 1 Hits* (London: Omnibus Press, 2005)

which was a hit with John. The disco-ish ELO-like "**Dreamin'**" was a hit in the fall and was at no. 10 in *Billboard* on the December 6, 1980, chart. "**Dreamin'**" was written by Leo Sayer, who was in the top 10 that week with a song he *didn't* write, "**More Than I Can Say.**" "**Dreamin'**" is Richard's last top 10 hit in the U.S. to date.

It's interesting to note that Richard was almost an exact contemporary of John's, having been born on October 14, 1940, just five days after John. However, Richard had a four-year head start on John as far as their recording careers went. Richard made the U.S. charts two years before the Beatles arrived when his version of "**It's All in the Game**" got to no. 25 in 1962. John once said that there was no worthwhile British rock prior to Richard's landmark 1958 recording of "**Move It.**"

Always a huge star in his homeland where he has sold more records than anyone except for the Beatles and Elvis, 1980 marked Richard's most successful year on the U.S. charts.

ALAIN GORAGUER

Soundtrack: *Planete Sauvage* aka *Fantastic Planet*

In a 2016 interview with *Mojo* Magazine, Sean Lennon shared his memo-
ries of his early childhood:

> "There were basically two videos that I watched as a kid –
> Planete Sauvage, this French sci-fi film that my dad loved,
> and (Disney's) Fantasia. I still listen to the Planete Sauvage
> soundtrack all the time, just to bring me back to a certain base
> level of what I thought was cool.[56]

*Fantastic Planet* (as the film was re-titled for U.S. release) is an animated film directed by Rene Laloux that told the allegorical tale of small,
human-like creatures being subjugated on a fictional planet by its giant
blue native inhabitants. The subtext is man's inhumanity to those he
deems to be inferior. It is a wildly inventive film and was honored with
the Special Award prize at the 1973 Cannes Film Festival. The film's animation, which was illustrated by Roland Topor, reminds a viewer of both
the Beatles' *Yellow Submarine* and Terry Gilliam's animated pieces for
*Monty Python's Flying Circus*, yet is unique. *Fantastic Planet* would appear
to have influenced the creators of *South Park* decades later.

*Fantastic Planet* was a staple at midnight movie showings during the
1970s and '80s. This was when mostly stoned theater patrons enjoyed

---

56    Alan Light, "The Mojo Interview: Sean Lennon" *Mojo* Magazine, July 2016

trippy movies like *Fantastic Planet* or outrageous ones like *The Rocky Horror Picture Show*[57] on the big screen.

It turns out John played an important role in instigating the phenomenon of midnight movie showtimes in the U.S. with his championing of Chilean director Alejandro Jodorowsky's (like Topor, a member of the Panic Movement which was founded in 1962 and conducted various surreal "happenings") 1970 film *El Topo*, which the director described as "LSD without LSD," while critics dubbed it an "acid western." John saw *El Topo* several times at the Elgin Theater[58] on Eighth Avenue in Greenwich Village where it was shown at midnight or later two nights a week in late 1970 into 1971. John loved *El Topo* so much that he convinced Allen Klein to acquire the U.S. distribution rights for ABKCO. Jodorowsky later said: "John Lennon told his manager to give me $1 million to do whatever I would like to create next."[59] (That turned out to be 1973's *The Holy Mountain*.) As in New York, *El Topo* was often shown at midnight in theaters around the U.S., inaugurating a practice that soon became common. John was also responsible for musician John Barnham recording a new **version** of *El Topo's* soundtrack, which was released on Apple Records.

Before composing the **soundtrack** to *Fantastic Planet*, Alain Goraguer had worked composing and arranging for French singers including Serge Gainsbourg and France Gall. Gall's recording of Gainsbourg's song **Poupee de Cire, Poupee de Son** (literally Wax Doll, Rag Doll, but the usual naughty Gainsbourg double entendres come into play here) was conducted by Goraguer and won the 1965 Eurovision Song Contest as

---

57  John and May Pang attended the L.A. premiere of the stage version, *The Rocky Horror Show*, at the Roxy in March 1974.

58  Since renamed the Joyce Theater.

59  "El Topo: The weirdest Western Ever Made" by Larushka Ivan-Zadeh bbc.com 7/23/20

Luxembourg's entry.

Befitting the animation that it accompanied, Goraguer's *Fantastic Planet* **soundtrack** is intriguing and inventive, combining guitars with wah-wah effects, a choir, mellotron, harpsichord and more to form a jazzy, psychedelic score somehow brings to mind both Pink Floyd (specifically ***Atom Heart Mother***) and sexploitation movie soundtracks of the era.

Sean's video for his cover of T. Rex's song Would I Be the One from his 2006 *Friendly Fire* album features his own animation and is a tribute to *Fantastic Planet*.

Sean seems to have hit his stride in middle age, releasing two well-received albums with The Lennon Claypool Delirium, his collaboration with Les Claypool of Primus. Like Garaguer's *Fantastic Planet* soundtrack, Sean's new music is creative and hard to categorize.

# SPRING

ALTHOUGH THEY HADN'T BEEN CONSIDERED a "singles band" since the days of Syd Barrett, Pink Floyd's **"Another Brick in the Wall (Part 2)"** was the no. 1 song in the U.S. for four weeks in March and April. Meanwhile, their album *The Wall* continued its astonishing run at no. 1 that started in January and continued into May. The Beatles were recording *Sergeant Pepper* at Abbey Road in early 1967 while Pink Floyd were there making their Syd Barrett-helmed first album, the landmark *The Piper at the Gates of Dawn*. We can speculate that seeing a band that were basically his contemporaries having such massive success in early 1980 might have helped spur John's decision to return to recording.

Blondie's **"Call Me"** dislodged **"Another Brick in the Wall (Part 2)"** on April 19 and it remained atop the chart for the next six weeks. Blondie was one of John's favorite groups. **"Call Me"** would go on to be the biggest song of the year in the U.S. per *Billboard*.

**"With You I'm Born Again,"** a duet sung by "Fifth Beatle" Billy Preston and Syreeta Wright was a top five hit in April. That must have come as good news to John who was always fond of Billy since he'd played on the **"Get Back/Don't Let Me Down"** single in 1969, becoming the only outside person ever credited on a Beatles record. Preston is uncredited on the *Abbey Road* tracks **"Something"** (which John said was his favorite on the album) and John's own **"I Want You/She's So Heavy."** Wright was the co-author of **"Signed, Sealed, Delivered (I'm Yours),"** **"If You Really Love Me,"** and the Spinners hit **"It's a Shame,"** all of which she wrote with her ex-husband, Stevie Wonder.

Old school R&B was also in the top 5 that April with Ray, Goodman & Brown's song **"Special Lady."** The group were formerly known as The Moments of **"Love on a One Way Street** fame. Bob Seger & the Silver Bullet Band's album *Against the Wind* held down the no. 1 spot in the

*Billboard* album chart for six weeks from early May until mid-June. Two songs from the album —**"Fire Lake"** and **"Against the Wind"**—made the U.S. top 10 when released as singles. Glenn Frey and Timothy B. Schmit sang backing vocals on **"Fire Lake."** Schmit sang lead on the Eagles hit that spring, the haunting **"I Can't Tell You Why,"** a song he co-wrote with bandmates Frey and Don Henley. Frey later named the song as one of his favorite Eagles songs.

In the U.K. The Jam hit no. 1 on March 22 with **"Going Underground"** b/w **"Dreams of Children,"** which would stay atop the chart for three weeks. Such was the band's popularity that the song entered the chart at no.1, a feat that hadn't been accomplished in six years. (Since you asked, the last time had been Slade's **"Merry Christmas Everybody."** Go figure.) Songwriter Paul Weller sings an angry, politically charged song that also manages to be incredibly catchy. Both in their music and in the way they dressed, The Jam paid homage to groups like The Who and The Kinks, but the political fire of "**Going Underground"** surely owes something to John's songs such as "Gimme Some Truth."

An attempt to rescue the American hostages in Teheran was called off on April 24. While abandoning the staging area in the northeast of Iran a helicopter crashed into a transport plane, killing eight service members. After having counseled patience and diplomacy for the first six months of the crisis, the failure was a humiliating defeat for President Carter, and one that likely sealed his doom at the ballot box in November.

April saw the beginning of the Mariel boatlift, a month's long mass emigration from Fidel Castro's Cuba, in which approximately 150,000 refugees would enter the U.S.

The Mount St. Helens volcano erupted in Washington state on May 18 killing fifty-seven people. It was that kind of year. The second movie in the eventually seemingly endless *Star Wars* franchise, *The Empire Strikes Back*, was released on May 21.

John journeyed to South Africa by himself in late May, staying in Johannesburg and keeping a low profile. There is a photo of him sitting by himself on the plane back to New York. Upon returning to the U.S. in early June, he was soon preparing to sail to Bermuda, a trip that seemed to help free him of the creative and spiritual malaise that seemed to have been engulfing him.

May 29 brought an unwanted echo of the 1960s when civil rights leader Vernon Jordan was the victim of an assassination attempt outside a hotel in Fort Wayne, Indiana. Serial killer and white supremacist Joseph Paul Franklin was tried and acquitted of the crime but later confessed to shooting Jordan prior to being executed for other murders. Franklin later also confessed to shooting *Hustler* magazine publisher Larry Flynt in Georgia in 1978, which left Flynt permanently paralyzed from his wounds. Jordan survived the shooting and later served as an advisor to his friend President Bill Clinton during the 1990s.

"**Funkytown** "by Lipps, Inc. was all over the radio and stayed atop the ***Billboard*** Hot 100 for four weeks in May and June. By the end of spring on June 21, John was hard at work in Bermuda, writing and demoing new songs in preparation for recording what would become ***Double Fantasy***.

## PAUL MCCARTNEY
*"Coming Up"* and *McCartney II*

John was already thinking about a return to music in early 1980, but several accounts suggest that it was hearing **"Coming Up"** was the critical moment that jarred him out of his lethargy, got his completive juices flowing, and compelled him to get back in the game. John once claimed that if he heard a good song on the radio, instead of just enjoying it, he saw it as a challenge to himself to do something even better. Apparently, that's exactly what happened when his listened to **"Coming Up."** The competition between Lennon and McCartney to keep one-upping each other when it came to songwriting was the engine that drove the Beatles, and it seems old habits died hard.

In his excellent book *Here, There and Everywhere* the Beatles long-time engineer Geoff Emerick made this intriguing observation about John:

> "Beneath all the bluff and bluster, John struck me as a very insecure person. I'm not sure what he had to be insecure about, unless it was the songwriting competition he was always engaged in with Paul. Perhaps deep down he thought that Paul was more talented than he was."[60]

Armchair psychology aside, it would seem that Paul had the ability to make John rise to an occasion in a way that no one else could.

---

60    Geoff Emerick and Howard Massey, *Here, There and Everywhere: My Life Recording the Music of the Beatles* (New York: Gotham Books, 2006).

JOHN LENNON : 1980 PLAYLIST

In April John was driving with his aide Fred Seaman[61] on Long Island while staying at his recently purchased Long Island home, Cannon Hill, in Cold Spring Harbor, NY. When Paul's new single "**Coming Up**" came on the radio, John listened and was impressed. So much so that he requested a copy of the new *McCartney II* album, which Seaman soon procured. Although Seaman writes that John found the record a hit or miss affair, he was impressed with the fact that Paul included some out-of-the-box experiments on the album, and found it an improvement over Paul's previous effort *Back to the Egg*. A note (likely from 1979)[62] was later found in which John requested that Seaman get him a copy of *Back to the Egg*. Despite the presence of one of the great McCartney rockers, "**Getting Closer**," Seaman reports that John pronounced the LP to be "junk." *Back to the Egg* would be the final Wings album.

The live "hit" version of "**Coming Up**" was recorded at the Glasgow Apollo in Scotland on December 17, 1979, at the tail end of Wings' British tour. It was released as the B-side to the album version 45, but U.S. dee-jays decided they and their listeners preferred the more rocked out live version. In the U.S. the live version was subsequently included as a bonus 45 with the *McCartney II* album. The live version of "**Coming Up**" hit no. 1 on the U.S. *Billboard* chart on June 28, and stayed there for three weeks. If you exclude two duets—1982's "Ebony and Ivory" with Stevie Wonder and 1983's "Say Say Say" with Michael Jackson—"**Coming Up**" remains Paul's last solo U.S. no. 1 to date.

John thought that Paul was something of a control freak, so he found it fitting that he played all the instruments on *McCartney II*, just as he had on his 1970 solo debut, *McCartney*. Paul's soon to be ubiqui-tous Yuletide single "**Wonderful Christmastime**" had been recorded in

---

61    Seaman

62    Davies, *Letters*

the same one-man-band manner and released months earlier, prior to Christmas 1979.

Hearing that Paul could hold his own on the 1980 music scene may have convinced John that there was no reason he couldn't also. Or perhaps he saw it as a challenge. As long as Paul was churning out with material like "**With a Little Luck**" or "**Goodnight Tonight**" (no. 5 U.S. in 1979) John could rest easy, but "**Coming Up**"—in its quirky studio and propulsive live versions—was another matter and appeared to get John's competitive juices flowing.

We know that John videotaped himself at Cannon Hill in April performing "**Dear Yoko**," which is in its complete form, so the pieces of the puzzle were starting to fall into place. This is likely the first demo recording of one of the *Double Fantasy* songs in which it appears in a form close to its album version.

Seaman's account of John's reaction to "**Coming Up**" is backed up by Tyler Coneys, who sailed to Bermuda with John in June. While preparing for the trip he was listening to the car radio with John while driving in Newport, Rhode Island, when "**Coming Up**" came on. "John heard that. I think that stirred him a little bit … that stuck in his head."[63] Asked about John's attitude toward Paul, George, and Ringo, Coneys said "There was no question [that] they liked each other. They were friends … all of them."[64] Coneys got the impression that John started wanting to write songs after that car ride. Of course, that's exactly what John did upon his arrival in Bermuda. In fact, one of the first songs he wrote there, "**I Don't Want to Face It**," has a guitar riff that mimics the horns on "**Coming Up**" and lyrics with lines that begin "You say...," just like Paul's song. Some have even construed "**I Don't Want to Face It**" as

---

63    *Bermuda Tapes* app

64    Ibid.

John's answer to Paul's "**Coming Up.**"

Logic and common sense would dictate that John would keep a close eye on how his former partner's career was progressing, and this is born both by people who interacted with John and by his own statements. While Paul's solo career got off to a sluggish start, he began to hit his stride with the 1973 Wings album *Red Rose Speedway* and especially its follow-up, *Band on the Run*. *Red Rose Speedway* gave Paul his first U.S. no. 1 album since his debut *McCartney* in 1970, and started a streak in which his next four albums would hit the top of the *Billboard* charts. When 1978's *London Town* made it to no. 2, it was only locked out of the top spot by the phenomenal success of the *Saturday Night Fever* soundtrack which was no. 1 in the U.S. for almost six months.[65]

John's professed reason for taking a hiatus from the music business in 1975 was so that he could care for his newborn son, Sean, who was born on October 9, 1975. One wonders if Paul's career resurgence in 1973-75 may have played a role in John's decision. Perhaps John was reluctant to engage with Paul in a battle for popularity he knew he was unlikely to win?

John was said to be fond of Paul and Wings' 1976 hit "**Silly Love Songs**," even suspecting that Paul had addressed the song to him. Despite complaints from some quarters that the song showcased Paul at his saccharine worst, the public agreed with John and "**Silly Love Songs**" topped the *Billboard* Hot 100 for a month during June and July of 1976. Filling out a questionnaire in 1976, John wrote the word "extraordinary" next to Paul's name.

When *Playboy* interviewer David Sheff [66] stated to John "Some people feel that none of the songs Paul has done alone don't come close to

---

65     John on the Bee Gees: "There is nothing wrong with the Bee Gees. They do a damn good job. There was nothing else going on then."

66     Sheff and Golson

the songs he came up with as a Beatle," John didn't take issue with the opinion, merely stating "Well, that's Paul." In defending his own ten-plus years of solo work, John mentions only two songs, "**Imagine**" and "**Love**," plus "Those *Plastic Ono Band* songs" that "Stand up to any songs that were written while I was a Beatle." John was a tough critic, but it's remarkable to hear him at this late juncture agreeing with the widely held thesis that the Beatles solo work—including his own—rarely measured up to what the Beatles had accomplished as a unit.

Elsewhere in the interview John stated that he thought "**Coming Up**" was "A good piece of work," but that he hadn't listened to all of *McCartney II*. He did, however say that he'd heard an additional song from the album on which he thought Paul "sounded depressed." This was almost certainly referring to "**Waterfalls**," an underrated ballad that was the second single released from *McCartney II*. In the lyric, McCartney expresses anxiety about the physical safety of his loved ones.

In what would prove to be his only videotaped interview during 1980, on October 10 John sat down at the Hit Factory with *Los Angeles Times* music critic Robert Hilburn. John told Hilburn that he preferred the "freaky-deaky" studio version of "**Coming Up**" found on *McCartney II* to the hit live version that was a no. 1 U.S. hit that summer. Perhaps John also enjoyed the video that accompanied the studio version of the song in which Paul dressed up as various members of a band including as his younger self circa 1964, playing his old Hofner bass. This was slyly appropriate considering that Paul played all the instruments on the studio recording. Note that the studio version of "**Coming Up**" was the hit in the U.K., where it went to no. 2 on the charts. Asked by Hilburn if he was surprised that "**Coming Up**" was so good, John said "no" and poignantly asked "How can you be surprised by your brother?"

Even more touching are the words John stated as he rode to the studio in the late afternoon of December 8, 1980. RKO Radio host Dave Sholin had just interviewed John and Yoko but took this opportunity to ask about John about his relationship with Paul. According to Sholin, John answered:

> "Well he's like a brother. I love him. Families—we certainly have our ups and downs and our quarrels. But at the end of the day, when it's all said and done, I would do anything for him. I think he would do the same for me."[67]

---

67    Sue Summers, "John Lennon's Last Day," *The Daily Mail,* December 5, 2010, https:// www.dailymail.co.uk/tvshowbiz/article-1335829/John-Lennon-NEW-eyewitness-account-30th-anniversary-Beatles-murder.html

MATUMBI
*Point of View*

According to Fred Seaman, John picked up a tape of Matumbi's[68] album upon the recommendation of a record store clerk while in Bermuda. *Point of View* features an appearance by noted DJ I-Roy.

Seaman later wrote that while rehearsing at the Dakota prior to recording **Double Fantasy,** John played his tape of Matumbi's album for the musicians as an example of the "reggae groove" he was going for on the songs **"Living on Borrowed Time"** and **"Beautiful Boy.** "John assigned side two of the album as "homework" for the musicians to study before sessions commenced. John was attempting to school the session men on how Matumbi smoothy integrated horns into their steady reggae groove. While recording **"Borrowed Time"** at the Hit Factory John was recorded saying that "there's a lot of R&B coming into (modern reggae). ...There's a guy called Matumbi doing some very interesting stuff as well." Although John is seemingly unaware that Matumbi is a group, the music has obviously made an impression on him.

Kicking off with the **title track**, Side 2 of *Point of View* also includes the songs **"Judy McQueen," "Ordinary Man," "Boy Oh Boy," "Things I Do for You,"** and **"Living in a Dream."** Although John emphasized the second side to his players, the entire album is pretty great. Matumbi's music captures reggae's feel-good vibes in a memorable way.

---

68    Although Seaman doesn't name the album title, *Point of View* was far more commercially successful than Matumbi's 1978 album *Seven Seals*, so it is very probable that *Point of View* is the Matumbi album John owned.

*Point of View* features the talents of singer/guitarist Dennis "Blackbeard" Bovell, today acknowledged as the father of British Dub Music. His collaborations with dub poet Linton Kwesi Johnson, starting with the 1978 album *Dread Beat an' Blood*—which Johnson later described as his attempt to capture the "anger and hope" of his generation as Margaret Thatcher began her ascendancy to power—are now considered classics. Johnson's dub poetry created a new genre of reggae and would later be seen as vital in the development of rap music. When Johnson compiled songs for his appearance on the BBC's "Desert Island Discs" in 2002, John's **"Imagine"** and Bob Marley's **"Redemption Song"** were among his selections.

Matumbi had a British hit in 1976 with its cover of Bob Dylan's *New Morning* track **"The Man in Me."** That recording was the most popular reggae song in the U.K. that year. Matumbi toured with Ian Dury and the Blockheads and in 1978 recorded two sessions for legendary and highly influential British deejay John Peel. That year Matumbi also recorded the theme song for the popular British television show *Empire Road*. The **title track** of *Point of View* was a top 40 U.K. in the fall of 1979. The band performed it on *Top of the Pops* that October and Concerts for the People of Kampuchea at London's Hammersmith Odeon in December 1979.

On Monday, August 18, Matumbi played a show not far from Manhattan at My Father's Place in Roslyn, NY. John was otherwise engaged doing a video shoot at the Hit Factory and didn't attend.

JERRY LEE LEWIS
"Great Balls of Fire"

John requested[69] a 45 of this 1957 rock classic in May 1980 list for Fred Seaman. It was likely going into his jukebox.

John had loved Lewis' music from the time he first time he heard **"Whole Lotta Shakin' Goin' On."** Lewis was a profound, if strangely unappreciated influence on the development of the Beatles music. Among the Jerry Lee associated songs the band performed before they were famous were **"Mean Woman Blues"** (which helped get pianist Duff Lowe into an early version band, due to the fact that he could play the arpeggio at the beginning of it), **"High School Confidential,"** "It'll Be Me," **"Whole Lotta Shakin' Goin' On," "Down the Line,"** "Jambalala," **"Livin' Lovin' Wreck," "When the Saints Go Marchin' In,"** "You Win Again," **"Fools Like Me,"** and **"Great Balls of Fire"**.

Lewis recorded his ***Live at the Star Club*** at the Beatles former Hamburg, Germany haunt backed by the Nashville Teens in 1964. It is unquestionably one of the greatest, and very possibly *the* greatest rock album of all time. Lewis exhibits a take no prisoners approach throughout the astonishing performance.

John paid a kind of tribute to Lewis at the Beatles first Shea Stadium concert on August 15, 1965, when, during **"I'm Down,"** he played the organ using some of Jerry's Lee's patented moves such as moving his elbow up and down the keyboard.

---

69    Davies, *Letters*

The Beatles performed "**You Win Again**," "**Whole Lotta Shaking Goin' On**," and "**Fools Like Me**" during the January 1969 *Get Back* sessions.

In explaining to *Playboy* that he didn't go out to see other performers John stated: "I might like Jerry Lee Lewis singing "**A Whole Lot of Shakin'**" on the record, but I'm not interested in seeing him perform it." Times had changed since October 1973 when John had gone to see Lewis at the Roxy Club in L.A. After the show John went to Lewis' dressing room, knocked, and without a word prostrated himself before "The Killer" and kissed his boots. Who else would get such treatment from John?

Elliot Mintz accompanied John that night and recalled that John watched in awe from the balcony as his musical hero performed. "He was looking at Jerry Lee the way a child would open a Christmas present." Mintz recalled that Lewis tried to dissuade John as he beheld one of the most famous men in the world smooching his footwear: "Now, now son that's not necessary."[70]

---

70    https://www.youtube.com/watch?time_continue=133&v=ME3xnEeV3C0&feature=
      emb_logo

## MADNESS
### "One Step Beyond"

Along with The Specials and The Selecter, Madness spearheaded the late 1970s "two-tone" ska revival in the U.K. Two-tone referred to combining elements of Jamaican ska and rock steady music—styles which would evolve into reggae—and combining them with the energy of punk rock.

Madness songs, likely including **"One Step Beyond"**, were on the tape that Fred Seaman gave to John in the spring of 1980. In his BBC interview, John singled out **"One Step Beyond"** as a favorite of the new wave songs he'd heard:

> "I'm aware of ... Madness. 'Don't do that. Do this.' (As on the spoken word intro to **"One Step Beyond"**.) I think that is the most original thing actually because it's so peculiar. ... Out of all that mob I think that was one of the most original sounds. Very good drumming, very good bass and all of that."[71]

**"One Step Beyond"** was a cover of a song that was originally the B-side of Prince Buster's song **"Al Capone"** in 1964. **"Al Capone"** did make the U.K. top 20, but not until 1967 when it went no. 18. The Madness version was released in October 1979 and was a hit in the U.K., where it got to no. 7, and in other European countries such as France where it was a no. 1 hit. Their album of the same name was a huge success

---

71    Lennon, Ono and Peebles. *The Last Lennon Tapes*, (New York: Dell, 1983)

in the U.K., getting no. 2 and staying on the album charts for over a year.

The memorable intro to **"One Step Beyond"** that made such an impression of John was spoken by Madness member Chas Smash aka Cathal "Carl" Smyth.

In 1964 the Beatles tried their hand at ska during the instrumental bridge of **"I Call Your Name"**. John later said "the solo on **"I Call Your Name"** was ska—deliberate and conscious."[72] **"I Call Your Name"** was an early composition of John's that was first recorded—not by the Beatles—but by Brian Epstein proteges Billy J. Kramer and the Dakotas in 1963. It served as the B-side to another "John" Lennon and McCartney song **"Bad to Me"**, which Kramer took to no. 1 in the U.K. that year. **"Bad to Me"** might be the best of the songs John and Paul "gifted" to other artists. Curiously, the Beatles recorded **"I Call Your Name"** almost a year later in March 1964 during sessions for *A Hard Day's Night*. This may have been because John thought the song deserved a better fate than to be relegated to a Billy J. Kramer's B-side. While recording the song, John asked George Martin if they were veering too close to Kramer's version.

It's worth noting that the Beatles recorded **"I Call Your Name"** in March 1964, two months before Millie Small recorded her worldwide smash **"My Boy Lollipop"**, the song that put ska on the map worldwide. As usual, they were setting trends, not following them.

Possibly due to its' similarity to **"You Can't Do That"** (both had John singing lead and featured the cowbell prominently), **"I Call Your Name"** was released in the U.K. on the *Long Tall Sally* EP instead of the *A Hard Day's Night* soundtrack album. In the U.S. it was included on *The Beatles Second Album*, a ramshackle affair that collected various U.K. hits and B-sides plus the *With the Beatles* songs left off the U.S.

---

72    Ibid

*Meet the Beatles* album. Got that?

The Mamas and the Papas covered **"I Call Your Name"** on their 1966 debut album *If You Can Believe Your Eyes and Ears*. Mama Cass—who had a thing for John—even whispers John's name during the instrumental break. Although not released as a single, this version of the song rivals the Beatles' own in terms of U.S. radio play.

**"I Call Your Name"** doesn't deserve its unheralded status in the Beatles catalog. It's also an important song in John's artistic development. He said this about the song in his *Playboy* interview:

> "It was one of my *first* attempts at a song. ... When there was no Beatles and no group. I just had it around. It was my effort as a kind of blues originally, and then I wrote the middle just to stick it in the album when it came out years later. The first part had been written before Hamburg (1960) even."[73].

Madness are best known in the U.S. for their 1983 hit "Our House."

---

73    Sheff and Golson

BILLY JOEL
"It's Still Rock and Roll to Me"
*Glass Houses*

As John was taking sailing lessons that spring on the waters near his home in Oyster Bay, Long Island, he was heard to shout "Where are you, Billy Joel? I love your album!"[74] Joel had a home nearby and John knew he was a neighbor. John was no doubt referring to *Glass Houses*, the cover of which showed Joel about to throw a rock through the windows of the house John was looking for. Both John and Joel had expressed a desire to meet each other at the time, but unfortunately, neither acted on it.

*Glass Houses* is a different sort of album for Joel. It's his response to New Wave with many of the songs featuring electric guitars, rather than Joel's piano. "**It's Still Rock and Roll to Me**" was #1 On *Billboard*'s Hot 100 singles chart for two weeks in late July 1980, just as John and Yoko were preparing for the start of the *Double Fantasy* sessions. It was Joel's first no. 1 single. *Glass Houses* was no. 1 on *Billboard*'s album chart for six weeks in June and July. It was ranked as *Billboard*'s fourth most popular album of 1980 and would go on to sell over seven million copies in the U.S. alone. "**You May Be Right**," the previous single from *Glass Houses*, had made it to #7 a few months earlier. Both songs were a ubiquitous presence on New York radio at the time.

"**Don't Ask Me Why**" channeled Paul McCartney and cracked the U.S. top 20 in the fall, but *Glass Houses*' standout tracks are "**All for**

---

74    Seaman.

Leyna" and "**Sometimes a Fantasy**," both convincing new wave style rockers that showcased Joel's versatility as a writer.

Joel is a long-time Beatlemaniac, an influence that usually showed up in his McCartney-esque ballads such as "**Just the Way You Are**" (a song of which John was especially fond and had on his jukebox) and "**She's Always a Woman**" from his breakthrough 1977 album *The Stranger*. His 1978 hit "**My Life**" features Beatle-inspired vocal harmonies in its bridge sections. Joel's 1982 album *The Nylon Curtain* wore its Beatle influences on its sleeve, notably on the Lennon-esque "Surprises," and "Scandinavian Skies."

In later years Joel has become friends with Paul McCartney. On July 18, 2008, Paul made a guest appearance at Joel's Shea Stadium concert, the last before the venue that loomed large in the Beatles' career met the wrecking ball, singing "**I Saw Her Standing There**" and "**Let it Be**." In a recent interview with Howard Stern, Joel discussed how he invited Paul to his home to get his take on one of Joel's recent compositions.

Is ***Double Fantasy*** a better album than ***Glass Houses***? It might be, but the answer is far from a slam dunk. Some would say it appeared the student had overtaken the teacher. As we will see, that may have been the case with Bruce Springsteen's "**The River**," also. Among those who believed that album outclassed ***Double Fantasy*** was John himself.

## DOLLY PARTON

"Great Balls of Fire" and "Starting Over Again"

Dolly's **"Great Balls of Fire"** single was released in August 1979. Somewhere around that time, John requested a copy of Dolly's 45 for his jukebox. The request provides further evidence not only of his eclectic tastes in music, but also that John was closely monitoring the music scene four years into his exile. Dolly turns in an excellent version of this Jerry Lee Lewis classic. Over a prominent horn section, Dolly rocks out in convincing fashion.

One wonders how John became aware of this song. Possibly from following the country charts in *Billboard* or perhaps listening to the New York country station of those days, WHN. Dolly's album of the same name contained a cover of **"Help."** She released **"Great Balls of Fire"** as a double A-side with **"Sweet Summer Lovin."**

Again, we see here that John had a soft spot for country music. Even before he learned to play guitar, John would sing Hank Williams's **"Honky Tonk Blues"** for fun. His 1957 business card for the Quarrymen listed:

"Country – Western – Rock 'n' Roll – Skiffle"

Set off by Lonnie Donegan's **"Rock Island Line,"** the U.K. skiffle craze compelled John to form his first band, the Quarrymen, in 1957. Skiffle was an amalgam of blues, folk, and country music that was played on conventional and improvised instruments, such as washboards.

In early 1975 John wrote to country singer Waylon Jennings[75] suggesting that he record John's song **"Tight A$"**, a rockabilly style number which had been released on ***Mind Games*** a year and a half earlier. It's amusing to see that one of the great songwriters of the century was still not below pitching his material to other artists. In his note, John seems to express regret that he'd never released **"Tight A$"** as a single himself. Indeed, **"Tight A$"** is that rare entity: an unheralded and unjustly neglected Lennon song. After the **title track**, **"Tight A$"** is easily the second-best song on ***Mind Games***. Still, Jennings didn't take John up on his suggestion, and he never recorded **"Tight A$"**.

One of the final songs John would compose in the second half of 1980 was **"Life Begins at Forty,"** a straight-up country song. The song includes an intro from John in which he uses a southern accent. Listening to it one is reminded of the Rolling Stones cod-country ***Some Girls*** track **"Faraway Eyes"**, which may be at least a subconscious reference point for John here. **"Life Begins at Forty"** was intended to be given to Ringo to record for his forthcoming album, *Can't Fight Lightening*. Ringo celebrated his fortieth birthday on July 7, 1980, three months after John hit the milestone on October 9. There were reportedly plans afoot for John to record with Ringo (and possibly Paul) in Los Angeles in early 1981. After John's death, Ringo found himself too distraught to attempt John's song, which had now taken on a sad irony. Ringo's album was retitled *Stop and Smell the Roses* and was released in September 1981. It featured songs from both Paul and George.

Dolly had broken into mainstream pop success in 1978 with her smash hit **"Here You Come Again."**

Dolly's **"Staring Over Again"** is the song that caused John to rename

75    Chip Madinger and Scott Raille, *Lennonology: Strange Days Indeed* (Chesterfield, MO, Open Books, 2015).

his song **"(Just Like) Starting Over"** to avoid confusion with Dolly's song. Dolly's **"Starting Over Again"** had gone to no. 1 on *Billboard's* County chart on May 24, 1980, so it was no obscurity. **"Starting Over Again"** is a pleasing country ballad typical of the day, when country was ascending in mainstream popularity. (This was the summer of *Urban Cowboy*, the movie that featured Johnny Lee's hit **"Looking for Love"** and helped bring country music into the mainstream.) Its lyrics describe the break-up of a marriage, the flip side of John's **"Starting Over"** which is suggesting a new start for a long-term relationship. Surprisingly, **"Starting Over Again"** was written by Donna Summer and her husband, Bruce Sudano. It features a typically sincere vocal from Dolly.

Dolly graced the cover of the December 11 issue of *Rolling Stone*, which would have hit the streets at the end of November. Her new song **"Nine to Five"** had been released on November 3 and was on its way to hitting the top of both the *Billboard* country and pop charts in early 1981.

# SUMMER

JOHN SPENT MOST OF JUNE and July in Bermuda. Newly inspired following his sailing trip to get there, he worked to craft new songs as the decision was taken to return to the studio to record, and spent time with Sean. John had the idea to record the album in Jamaica, and even thought of making a trip to explore studios there, but it never happened.

In the U.S. frustration rose as the Iranian hostage crisis dragged on. The Republican National Convention in July nominated Ronald Reagan for president and former CIA director George Bush for vice president, setting them up to face President Carter and Vice President Walter Mondale in November, with Illinois Republican Congressman John Anderson running as an independent third-party candidate. Reagan's seemingly innocuous selection of Bush as his running mate would prove to have profound implications for U.S. and world politics in the coming decades, with both Bush (1989-93) and his son George W. (2001-09) going on to serve as U.S. president. In a nod to his evangelical Christian supporters, Reagan took the unusual step of ending his convention acceptance speech with a moment of silent prayer. Accused by his detractors of being trigger-happy and an intellectual lightweight, years of movie and television appearances had made Reagan an expert at presenting himself before a camera, and opponents who underestimated him would do so at their peril.

The Democratic Convention took place at Madison Square Garden from August 11-14. Just fifteen blocks up Eighth Ave. John and Yoko were recording **Double Fantasy**.

Proving that nostalgia for the 1960s had its limits, Carter ended up defeating Ted Kennedy by a six-hundred vote margin. In his concession speech marking the end of his first and what would prove to be his last presidential campaign, Kennedy delivered a valedictory for the optimistic spirt of the 1960s embodied by his assassinated brothers, declaring: "The cause endures, hope still lives, and the dream shall never die."

Kennedy's refusal to concede prior to the convention and reluctance to grant Carter more than a perfunctory handshake on the dais helped seal the incumbent president's fate in November. Carter's convention acceptance speech in which he referred to recently departed former Vice President Hubert Horatio Humphrey as "Hubert Horatio *Hornblower*," after the fictionalized character created by C.S. Forester didn't help.

The first tears in the Iron Curtain across eastern Europe were made that summer in the unlikely locale of Gdansk, Poland, where electrician Lech Walesa led workers' Solidarity union strike which resulted in government recognition of the first independent union in a Warsaw Pact country. This would set the ball rolling on the eventual demise of the Soviet Union later in the decade. Walesa went on to win the Nobel Peace Prize and to become the first democratically elected president of Poland in 1990.

As we shall see, Paul McCartney and the Rolling Stones both topped the U.S. charts that summer, Paul with his "**Comin' Up**" single, and the Stones with their album ***Emotional Rescue***. Another contemporary of John's, The Who's Pete Townsend, had top 10 *Billboard* single with "**Let My Love Open the Door**," a song he described as mere "ditty."

AC/DC released their landmark album ***Black in Black*** on July 25. It was their first album with new lead singer Brian Johnston, who replaced Bon Scott after Scott died in February. A highly influential album considered by many to be the best hard rock album of all time, ***Back in Black***'s songs "**Hell's Bells**" and "**You Shook Me All Night Long**" were played on WNEW-FM in New York upon the album's release and were likely heard by John since he had the station playing during down time at the Hit Factory.

The run of classic R & B during the year continued when the

Manhattan's old school ballad "**Shining Star**" go to no. 5 on the U.S. *Billboard* singles chart in August.

On August 23rd, the Heatwave Festival, featuring many top new wave bands, was held at Mosport Park in Ontario, Canada. The festival was the brainchild of promoter John Brower, who had invited John and to perform at the Toronto Rock and Roll Festival back in September 1969. That performance, with Yoko and the Plastic Ono Band with Eric Clapton on guitar, was preserved for posterity on the *Live Peace in Toronto* album. Over 100,000 fans showed up for the Heatwave Festival, strong testament to the popularity of new wave at the time. John was a fan of many of the bands performing that day including the B-52s, the Pretenders, Rockpile, and Elvis Costello. (The Clash were supposed to headline Heatwave, but didn't arrive due to immigration problems.) Talking Heads played with an expanded, funkier lineup that included ex-Labelle[76] singer Nona Hendrix and keyboardist Bernie Worrell. They played songs – including **Once in a Lifetime** – from their Brian Eno pro-duced new album *Remain in Light*, which would be released on October 10th and go on to be cited as the best album of 1980 in many year-end surveys. As noted earlier, while in Bermuda John recorded himself sing-ing **Take Me to the River**, an Al Green song that Talking Heads had popularized when they recorded their brilliant cover of it in 1978.

John returned to New York on August 28, just as the city's newspa-pers were filled with stories about the murder of a young violinist named Helen Hagnes at the Metropolitan Opera House during a break in a per-formance by the Berlin Ballet. She had been thrown to her death from the roof of the building and the tabloids dubbed the case "The Murder at the Met." Fear that the murderer would strike again was rampant in the city (this was only three summers removed from the Son of Sam case) until

76    A French television show filmed John singing LaBelle's hit song **Lady Marmalade** while accompanying himself on piano in the spring of 1975.

a stagehand was arrested in late August and later convicted. "The Met" was and is located in Lincoln Center, just eight blocks down Columbus Ave. from the Dakota, so one can assume that John was among the many New Yorkers keeping track of the case.

THE B-52S

"Rock Lobster"

**"Rock Lobster"** is one of the most consequential songs in this book because, upon hearing it at a club called Disco 40 in Hamilton, Bermuda, in June, John called Yoko and told her to start planning recording sessions for a new album that would become ***Double Fantasy***.

John later told the BBC what he thought upon hearing "**Rock Lobster**" for the first time:

> "That's Yoko! I thought there were two records going at once of something. Because it was so her. I mean, this person (Kate Pierson) had *studied* her. I thought, 'Get the ax (guitar) and call the wife.' I called her and said 'You won't believe this, but I was in a disco and there was somebody doing your voice. This time they're ready for us."[77]

Featuring kitschy early 1960s throwback elements like a Farfisa organ and a very cool surf guitar line, "**Rock Lobster**" stood out as something new and different in the musical world of 1979-80. The beehive hairdos on Kate Pierson and Cindy Wilson also upped the band's camp factor, as did singer Fred Schneider's unusual vocal stylings. Proving that John's ears hadn't failed him, Pierson and Wilson later revealed that they were consciously imitating Yoko vocally on "**Rock Lobster**."

---

77    Lennon, Ono, Peebles

The B-52s got their start in Athens, Georgia, home to a thriving music scene due to the presence of the University of Georgia campus. The newly christened R.E.M.—soon to be the most important American band of the 1980s—played their first gig in Athens that April.

John was a little late to the party as far as "**Rock Lobster**" was concerned. The song had been released on the group's debut album *The B-52s* in July 1979. "**Rock Lobster**" was a popular track on rock radio during the rest of 1979, and remains so until this day, especially during the summer. The B-52s performed the song during their appearance on *Saturday Night Live* on January 26, 1980. John, a regular viewer of *SNL*, would appear to have missed this episode, which opened with extensive "Weekend Update" coverage of Paul McCartney's marijuana bust in Japan.

The cynical amongst us might question the disco story as being a cog in the possibly dubious narrative that John had rediscovered his lost muse during his sailing trip to Bermuda. Although a close observer like Fred Seaman found John reinvigorated and working hard on new material in Bermuda, we also know that several of the *Double Fantasy* songs had been around for years prior to 1980. For instance, in her 1983 book *Loving John*,[78] May Pang writes that John was working on the melody to what would eventually evolve into "**Beautiful Boy**" in early 1975. "**I Don't Wanna to Face it**" originated in 1977, and both "**Starting Over**" and "**Watching the Wheels**" had gestated for at least a year or more. "**I'm Losing You**" began life as "**Stranger's Room**," which likely dates from 1978. Yoko set the record straight in 2007 when she told the BBC that from 1975 to 1979: "(John) was writing some songs but he wasn't that pleased with what he was writing."[79]

---

78    Pang

79    BBC, *Desert Island Discs* with Yoko, June 10, 2007.

Taking bits of earlier songs and placing them in new ones had always been part of John's songwriting process. Given his status as one of the greatest songwriters of the 20th century, it seems like he used this technique quite successfully! Whatever the timeline, the demos John recorded in Bermuda would provide the musical blueprint for the ***Double Fantasy*** sessions.

Nevertheless, it appears that hearing "**Rock Lobster**" that night played at least some role in the decision to schedule studio time back in New York to record a new album. Therefore, the fact that the B-52s were "doing" Yoko apparently played a role in determining that the time was right for Yoko's music thus giving impetus to make the new album a joint John and Yoko project.

Yoko confirmed this in a 2013 *Songfacts* interview:

> "Listening to the B-52s, John said he realized that my time had come. So he could record an album by making me an equal partner and we won't get flack like we used to up to then."[80]

In February 2002 Yoko joined the B-52s onstage to perform "**Rock Lobster**." Whatever else you want to say about the B-52s, there aren't many bands that can say they inspired John Lennon to record an album.

Perhaps we shouldn't be surprised that John found renewed inspiration in the Caribbean. One of the first songs he ever wrote was called "**Calypso Rock**." John owned a copy of the early Lord Kitchener album ***Calypsos Too Hot to Handle***, and according to Fred Seaman, was able to correctly identify a song as being sung by "Calypso King of the World" Mighty Sparrow when it came over the radio in the spring of 1980.[81]

---

80    Greg Prato, "Yoko Ono," Songfacts, https://www.songfacts.com/blog/interviews/yoko-ono

81    Seaman

## THE WAILERS
*Burnin'*

## BOB MARLEY AND THE WAILERS
*Survival* and *Uprising*

According to Fred Seaman's account,[82] John spent an evening in Bermuda getting high and listening to Bob Marley & the Wailers albums. As one does.

*Burnin'* was one of John's favorite albums since the time of its release in 1973. It was credited to "The Wailers" and is the last album Marley made with Bunny Livingston and Peter Tosh. Critic Robert Christgau wrote of *Burnin'*: "What's inescapable is Bob Marley's ferocious gift for melodic propaganda."[83]

John loved the *Burnin'* song "**Get Up, Stand Up**" so much that he played it for his *Double Fantasy* session musicians when they were recording "**Borrowed Time**" in August. John describes the track as having the "most beautiful rhythm" and adds "I just wanted you to hear something beautiful" before returning to work on "**Borrowed Time**." He points out the subtleties in the Wailers' sound beyond the "ching ching" reggae rhythm. John indicates that he prefers *Burnin'* to Marley's later work. In describing the feel he wanted on "Borrowed Time," John refers the musicians to the Isley Brothers tracks "**Twist and Shout**" and "**Spanish Twist**."

82    Seaman

83    Robert Christgau, Consumer Guide 1970s, www.robertchristgau.com

Speaking of "**Borrowed Time**," the *Burnin'* track "**Hallelujah Time**" was an important song to John. The lyric "Living on borrowed time" struck a chord with him and compelled him to complete a song on which he'd been working and name it "**Borrowed Time**." Surprisingly, "**Hallelujah Time**" was not written by Marley, Tosh, or Livingston, but by Bunny's wife, Jean Watt. Watt also contributed "**Pass it on**" to *Burnin'*. In addition to designing the Wailers stage outfits in the early days, she holds the distinction of being one of the few artists to inspire one of John's songs.[84]

Marley was wounded in an attempted assassination on December 3, 1976, almost four years to the day of John's death. Perhaps inevitably, Marley had been dragged into the bitter fight between Jamaica's two rival political parties, both of which coveted his endorsement.[85] Days after being shot Marley courageously performed as scheduled at a concert in which opposition leader Edward Seaga and socialist Prime Minister Michael Manley joined hands with him in a show of unity. Marley soon fled Jamaica for the U.K. Marley makes reference to the shooting incident on the *Survival* song "**Ambush in the Night**." *Survival* was released in 1979 and John played it a lot during his stay in Bermuda, according to Seaman. The album includes the songs "**Zimbabwe**,"[86] "**One Drop**," and its lead-off track "**So Much**

---

84    Jean Watt was reported missing from her Kingston home in May 2020.

85    The 2018 Netflix documentary *Remastered: Who Shot the Sheriff?* delves into the murky circumstances behind the shooting.

86    The new African nation of Zimbabwe was established on April 18, 1980. It emerged from the white-minority ruled Rhodesia, and Marley—whose music was widely played throughout Africa—had written "**Zimbabwe**" in support of that armed struggle. Marley and the Wailers played at the Independence Day ceremonies in what is now Harare (then Salisbury) before a crowd of tens of thousands, cementing his role as the preeminent world symbol of Pan-Africanism. Stevie Wonder made reference to Zimbabwean independence in his Marley tribute "**Master Blaster (Jammin')**" later that year.

**Trouble in the World."** With the flags of African nations on the cover underscoring the message of the song **"Africa Unite,"** *Survival* was a far more political work than its predecessor, 1978's *Kaya*, the title track of which concerns ganja. *Kaya* also boasts the straight-up love song **"Is This Love?"**

*Uprising* was brand-new at this time, having been released in the U.S. on June 10. It would be the last Marley album issued during his lifetime.

Notable songs on *Uprising* include **"Coming in From the Cold,"** **"Forever Loving Jah,"** and **"Could You Be Loved."** Most of the songs on the album were centered around Marley's Rastafarian beliefs, an understanding of which requires a knowledge of the brutal history of racism and subjugation of blacks in Jamaica.

John had been enthusiastic lover of reggae music for years. Prior to leading Elephant's Memory on his song **"Give Peace a Chance"** on the Jerry Lewis Labor Day weekend MDA Telethon in 1972, John shouts "Reggae baby! This is how they do it in Jamaica ... and London." The previous week they'd played the song the same way at the "One to One" benefit concert held at Madison Square Garden. That show is captured on the *Live in New York City* album and video.

John tried his hand at a reggae rhythm in 1973 on **"Mind Games."** He later complained that "trying to explain to American musicians what reggae was in 1973 was pretty hard." **"Mind Games"** was the standout track on John's otherwise lackluster album of the same name, and one of the finest songs of his entire solo career.

The year before that, John had been frustrated when recording Yoko's reggae-inflected *Some Time in New York City* track **"Sisters O Sisters."** John later told the BBC:

"I remember that session because (backing band) Elephant's Memory, all New York kids … saying they didn't know what reggae was. I'm trying to explain to them all, the only lick I knew to teach them was the 'Israelites' (no.1 in the U.K., no. 9 U.S. in 1969), that Desmond Dekker thing—so if you listen to it you'll hear me trying to get them to reggae."[87]

Nevertheless, "Sisters O Sisters" turned out to be a great track, and arguably among the best things Yoko ever recorded.

During the soon to commence *Double Fantasy* preparations, John would again be trying to teach American musicians how to play reggae.

John missed a last chance to see Marley and the Wailers in concert when they played at Madison Square on September 19 and 20 on an intriguing bill where they were preceded onstage by young rapper Curtis Blow—then riding the success of his Gold single "The Breaks"—and followed by the Commodores. *New York Times* critic Robert Palmer noted Marley's ability to win over the diverse crowd, describing his performance as "spellbinding." These two shows were the penultimate stop on Marley's U.S. tour, which declining health forced him to abandon following a last show in Pittsburgh on the 23. That show was released officially in 2011 and titled *Live Forever, September 23, 1980, Stanley Theater Pittsburgh, PA.* It's a truly remarkable document that features a moving performance of "Redemption Song," and the last song Marley ever sang onstage, "Get Up, Stand Up."

One of Marley's most powerful songs, "Redemption Song" is an unusually spare recording on which Marley is accompanied only by his acoustic guitar. The lines about freeing oneself from "mental slavery" were taken from a 1937 speech given by black nationalist leader Marcus

---

87    Lennon, Ono, Peebles

Garvey. **"Redemption Song"** is the final song on *Uprising*, and thus, in a sense, Marley's final artistic statement. It was written at a time when Marley's health had already taken a turn for the worse with a cancer diagnosis. The song asks: "How long shall they kill our prophets while we stand aside and look?"

Marley was only thirty-six when he died on May 11, 1981. With his death music had lost two of its most socially conscious voices within the space of a mere six months. But John and Marley shared an even more profound bond. As music critic Robert Christgau perceptively wrote not long ago: "Only the Beatles and conceivably Elvis Presley can claim as seismic a worldwide social effect (as Marley)."[88]

---

88    Christgau, Robert "Stateside Sufferation" in Williams, Richard, Editor *Exodus: Exile 1977* (London: Weidenfeld & Nicolson, 2017)

---

## ROCKY BURNETTE
"Tired of Toein' the Line"

Rocky is the son of one of John's musical heroes, Memphis-bred rocka-billy star Johnny Burnette. Documentation is scant, but it's almost certain that John knew of this likable song. Hearing **"Tired of Toein' the Line"** would have affirmed John's belief that the rock and roll music of his youth was back in fashion. Like John's **"(Just Like) Starting Over,"** Rocky's song combines classic elements with modern production techniques.

**"Tired of Toein' the Line"** peaked at no.8 in the U.S. *Billboard* Hot 100 for the week of July 26. This was the same week that John returned from Bermuda.

John and the Beatles had numerous Burnette connections starting with John's infatuation with the album ***Johnny Burnette and the Rock and Roll Trio***, which was released in 1956. John loved the album because every song was excellent. The record contained **"The Train Kept a-Rollin,"** memorably covered by the Yardbirds in the 1960s and Aerosmith in the 1970's; **"Honey Hush"**89, a Big Joe Turner cover which the Beatles recorded during the *Get Back* sessions in 1969; and **"Lonesome Tears in My Eyes,"** a song written by Johnny's brother Dorsey that the Beatles recorded for the BBC in 1963 with John on lead vocal. In addition, Ringo topped the U.S. *Billboard* singles chart with his cover of Johnny Burnette's 1960 solo hit **"You're Sixteen."** (Mr. Starkey was 33 years old at the time. Yes, things were different then!) Paul McCartney either

---

89    Paul McCartney would later recall John playing the Trio's **"Honey Hush"** first thing in the morning at the latter's ramshackle Gambier Terrace apartment in Liverpool.

plays the kazoo or imitates one with his voice during the solo on Ringo's **"You're Sixteen."**

In August 1964 Johnny Burnette drowned following a boating accident on Clear Lake, north of San Francisco. What are the chances that two of the most talented rock 'n roll performers of the 1950s die way before their time in a place called Clear Lake?

Rocky grew up in Memphis, and it wasn't unusual to have houseguests like Elvis, Eddie Cochran, and Gene Vincent in his home. He began his career as a songwriter and had his tunes recorded by the Osmonds and David Cassidy. In 1982 Rocky put together a new version of his dad's Rock and Roll Trio with original bassist Paul Burlison.

**"Tired of Toein' the Line"** was recorded at Rockfield Studios in Wales. It was co-written by Rocky and is on his appropriately titled album *Son of Rock 'n Roll*.

## THE SELECTER

*"Too Much Pressure"*

Along with The Specials and Madness, The Selecter were the leaders of the U.K. ska revival in 1979 and 1980. John was a fan of the three bands, all of which recorded for the Two-Tone label.

Fred Seaman reported[90] that while John and Yoko were rehearsing their songs at the Dakota on Monday, August 4, they got into a debate over Yoko's song "**Kiss, Kiss, Kiss**." John had the idea that the song would benefit if it was put to a ska beat like the one he'd heard on "**Too Much Pressur**e." While the tape of "**Too Much Pressure**" (from the **album** of the same name) blasted from a boombox, John tried to recreate the song's frantic beat on his drum machine. The effort was all for naught, as Yoko vetoed the idea of imitating the song's rhythm. While "**Kiss, Kiss, Kiss**" wasn't recorded with a ska beat during the ***Double Fantasy*** sessions, it did have a very fast tempo and was probably Yoko's most successful contribution to the album.

Guitarist Earl Slick later commented that while Yoko's material was sometimes "out there," he enjoyed playing her songs because they gave him the opportunity to play the more experimental style of guitar he'd played on David Bowie's ***Station to Station*** album, whereas John's songs did not lend themselves to that type of playing.

Led by songwriter Neol Davies and singer Pauline Black, The Selecter burst on the scene in 1979, when their song "**The Selecter**" was

---

90    Seaman

the B-side of The Special AKA's (also known as "The Specials") song "**Gangsters**" and the record got to no. 6 on the U.K. charts. The Selecter released their own single, "**On My Radio** b/w *Too Much Pressure*" later that year, and it got to no. 6.

The tape that John had, *Too Much Pressure*, was released in February 1980. As we've seen, John had a long-term love affair with Jamaican music, and the affair was still going strong in 1980.

## LENE LOVICH

*Stateless* and "Lucky Number"

Although John mangled her name by referring to her as "Lenny Loveritch"—a clever twist from the man who authored *In His Own Write*, John was familiar enough with Lovich's work to request a copy of *Stateless* just as the **Double Fantasy** sessions were gearing up at the beginning of August. In addition to working on the arrangements for his own songs, John, as co-producer of the album, was concerned with how the band would work up Yoko's more unconventional material. Like the B-52s, Lovich was an admirer of Yoko's work, so John thought *Stateless* would provide pointers on how such songs could be presented in a modern, commercially successful form. While rehearsing Yoko's song "**I'm Your Angel**" at home, a frustrated John played a tape of *Stateless* and told Yoko: "When you hear this you'll understand why you can't get away with your stuff."[91]

Lovich's exotic look—combined with a European accent she utilized on certain songs—belied the fact that, like Chrissie Hynde of the Pretenders, Lovich was an American living as an expatriate in the U.K. Lene hailed from Detroit, Chrissie was from Ohio.

Lovich found success with her fairly conventional cover of Tommy James and the Shondell's 1967 hit "**I Think We're Alone Now**", and her own song "**Lucky Number**." Both songs are on *Stateless*, which was released in the U.K. in October 1978 and, after undergoing a remix, in

---

91    Seaman

the U.S. in 1979. Released as a single in January 1979, "**Lucky Number**" had an unusual sound for the time and went on become a top 5 hit in the U.K., Australia, and other countries. Even today, "**Lucky Number**" is one of the songs most associated with New Wave music. In New York both songs were heard often on the well-established rock station, WNEW-FM, and especially on WPIX-FM, which was featuring a more adventurous new wave format at the time.

Two other *Stateless* songs—"**Home**" and "**Say When**"—also got considerable airplay on U.S. radio.

Lovich recorded for Stiff Records in the U.K. In addition to Ian Dury, Stiff was also home to other artists John liked including Elvis Costello, Dave Edmunds, and Nick Lowe. *Stateless* even includes her cover of Lowe's pop gem "**Tonight**" from his 1978 album with two great titles —*Pure Pop for Now People* (U.S.) and *Jesus of Cool* (U.K.).

In listening to "**Lucky Number**," John may have noted that although Lovich does a vocalization or two that are reminiscent of Yoko's work, for the most part the song sounds like traditional pop behind a new wave façade. This may be why the Yoko songs on *Double Fantasy* are far more accessible than most of her work on her previous albums had been. *Double Fantasy* was the first time since 1972's *Some Time in New York City* that John's and Yoko tracks had graced the same album.[92] Throughout the sessions, John worked hard to present Yoko's songs in a way that would gain her the mainstream recognition he thought she deserved.

When the word was out that John and Yoko were reviewing lucrative offers from record company moguls to decide which one would release their newly recorded music, they received a telegram from Stiff that read:

---

92   Yoko songs were, however, typically on the B-sides of John's early solo 45s.

"Heard you are recording. We're prepared to offer five-thousand dollars to sign with us."[93]

John thought it was funny.

In 1979 Stiff signed a Staten Island, New York band named Dirty Looks, who released their self-titled debut album on the label in 1980. Did John ever hear their great song "**Let Go**," which was played a bit on New York radio that summer? Here's hoping he did. Inspirational verse: "Don't you know that rock and roll is still the best drug?"

---

93    Ken Sharp, *Starting Over: The Making of John Lennon and Yoko Ono's Double Fantasy* (New York: Gallery Books, 2010)

✦ ✦ ✦

## A NOTE TO HIS MUSICIANS:

Reinvigorated by the trip sailing to Bermuda, John spent his time   there working hard to write and record the songs that formed the basis of **Double Fantasy** and **Milk and Honey**. Part of this process was repurposing fragments of old songs into new songs. The subsequent release of the many home demos John recorded in the latter years of his life has allowed scholars to precisely trace the origins of many of these songs. This was nothing new for John who had long had a policy of not "wasting the bits" of songs he'd come up with.

Upon his arrival back in New York on Monday, July 28, John and Yoko immediately began organizing the recording sessions under vows of silence from all concerned. According to producer Jack Douglas, this was because John was unsure that he still "had it" and wanted to be able pull the plug on the project without news of it becoming public if he thought the recordings weren't up to his standards.

In full page, handwritten instructions, John referenced a number of songs—both of his own and by other artists—in describing the sounds he was going for on the tracks that were to be recorded for **Double Fantasy**. He explicitly notes on the bottom "All notes refer to SOUND only." In other words, doesn't want them to copy the music. The songs referenced are an intriguing window into John's eclectic musical tastes and how he, at least at the outset of the sessions, envisioned his new songs would be recorded. He is likely referring to his Bermuda demo tape, and not the final album, and he lists the songs by number and by "side 1" and "side

2." The decision had already been made that half the songs would be Yoko's before recording began.

The note is a fascinating document that surfaced as part of the *John Lennon: The New York City Years* exhibition staged in 2009 at the Rock and Roll Hall of Fame Annex in New York.

The songs are listed as follows. "Side One" has "**Beautiful Boy**," "**Stepping Out**," "**Wo/man**" (John's spelling), "**Borrowed Time**," "**I'm Losing You**," "**Dear Yoko**," "**Grow Old with Me**" (for which John suggests "brass or strings or both and maybe 'bagpipes'"), and "**Watching the Wheels**."

"Side Two" lists the songs "**Real Love (Waiting for You)**," "**Nobody Told Me (Everybody's Talking)**," and "**I Don't Wanna Face It**."

Its presence on this list proves that John intended to record "**Real Love**" for *Double Fantasy*, at least as the sessions were starting. The subtitle was probably an alternate title. John put a lot of work in on "**Real Love**," recording six demos as he perfected it. It grew out of a song called "**Real Life**," which was also the source of the intro to "**(Just Like) Starting Over**." The fact that John says he plans on putting "strings etc." on it might explain why it wasn't recorded in the studio that summer. The three surviving Beatles overdubbed their voices and instruments onto one of John's "**Real Love**" demos for the *Anthology* project in the mid-1990s with gratifying, if strangely unheralded, results.

Like "**Real Love**," "**Grow Old with Me**" was never recorded during the *Double Fantasy* sessions, possibly because John had planned to give it a more elaborate arrangement than the rest of the songs being recorded. (Interestingly, engineer Tony Davilio later published[94] a handwritten list of "songs we recorded during *Double Fantasy*" that *does* include "**Grow Old with Me**." At the very least this would indicate that Davilio had

---

94    Tony Davilio with Mary Vicario *The Lennon Sessions* (Victoria, B.C.: Trafford: 2004.)

prepared an arrangement for the song.) On the other hand, Yoko's "**Hard Times Are Over**" had a choir overdubbed onto it in September, so maybe there's another explanation, such as not wanting to have too many slow songs on the album or time considerations—the album needed to be out well before Christmas. Both "**Real Love**" and "**Grow Old with Me**" are surely better songs than the more upbeat "**Cleanup Time**," which did make the album.

The songs referenced by John in his note are as follows:

## MONTY ALEXANDER
"Jamento"

John referenced the Jamaican jazz pianist's 1978 hit **"Jamento"** in describing how the piano on **"Beautiful Boy (Darling Boy)"** should interact with a steel drum. Monty Alexander is a Jamaican jazz pianist rooted in the classics of greats like Duke Ellington and Thelonious Monk. John's familiarity with his work provides further proof not only of the breadth of his taste in music, but also that he was keeping abreast of what was going on in music even during the secluded house-husband years.

A native of Kingston, Jamaica, Alexander was still a teenager when Frank Sinatra saw him performing at a Miami club in 1962 and invited him to be the pianist at his personal hangout, a club in midtown Manhattan named Jilly's, which was operated by his close pal, Jilly Rizzo. Alexander has lived in New York for many years, often performing in the city's many fine jazz clubs. Upon his arrival, he was soon making friends with jazz luminaries like Milt Jackson and Miles Davis. John's longstanding love of Jamaican music is well documented (SEE: Madness—**"One Step Beyond"**) so it's not surprising that he would be up on Alexander's music.

**"Jamento"** is the breezy title track to Alexander's 1978 album. It was composed by Alexander and features the guitar work of Jamaican musical *Zelig*, Ernest Ranglin, who often played on Alexander's albums. Ranglin's singular contributions to Jamaican music include arranging Millie Small's **"My Boy Lollipop,"** the song that brought the music to worldwide attention for the first time in 1964; establishing his own popularity with U.K. fans in the mid-'60s when he often played at Ronnie Scott's prestigious jazz club in London, serving as musical director for the recording of the Melodians' 1967 hit "**Rivers of Babylon**," and playing guitar in Jimmy Cliff's touring band in the 1970s. Note that photographer Bob Gruen remembers attending a Cliff show with John in New York, probably in the mid 1970s, so it is likely John saw Ranglin perform with Cliff at that time. John produced Harry Nilsson's cover of Cliff's hit "**Many Rivers to Cross**" along with the rest of Harry's *Pussy Cats* album in 1974. Around 1979 John taped a home demo of himself performing "**Many Rivers to Cross**."

In the end, George Small's piano part on "**Beautiful Boy (Darling Boy)**"—suggested to him by John—is less prominent than the steel drum part that dominates the recording, giving it a Caribbean lilt.

## JERMAINE JACKSON
"Let's Get Serious"

In his instructions John references this current hit by Michael Jackson's older brother Jermaine. For his song **"I'm Stepping Out"** John specifies "Heavy Bass/guitar ala '**Let's Get Serious**' Germaine (sic) Jackson." John's awareness of "**Let's Get Serious**" is strong evidence that he was keeping a watchful eye (ear?) on the current music scene as he prepared to record his comeback album.

Michael Jackson was also on the U.S. singles chart that month with **"She's Out of My Life,"** the fourth hit single—following **"Don't Stop 'Til You Get Enough,"** **"Rock with You,"** and **"Off the Wall"**—from Jackson's massively successful *Off the Wall* album, which was released in August 1979. By this time Michael Jackson was well on his way to becoming the biggest musical phenomenon in the world during the 1980s.

"**Let's Get Serious**" was co-written especially for Jermaine by Stevie Wonder. Besides playing drums, piano, guitar, and synthesizer on the song, one-man band Stevie also sings lead on the bridge sections in addition to duetting with Jermaine. Stevie recorded the track to which Jermaine later overdubbed his vocals while Stevie served as producer.

"**Let's Get Serious**" topped the *Billboard* R&B chart for six weeks in May and June 1980. That made it the most successful song involving Wonder on the R&B chart since his 1970 hit "**Signed, Sealed, Delivered (I'm Yours)"** (which he also wrote with Lee Garrett, the co-writer of "**Let's Get Serious**") likewise spent six weeks at no. 1. You might say that

"**Let's Get Serious**" is the best Stevie Wonder song that's not a Stevie Wonder song.

Stevie outdid himself later in the year when his Bob Marley tribute "**Master Blaster (Jammin')**" topped the *Billboard* R&B chart for seven weeks, besting the run of "**Let's Get Serious**" on the same chart by a week. John kept abreast of the R & B scene by listening to WBLS-FM in New York.

In describing for *Playboy* how he was inspired to write "**Beautiful Boy**" for his son, Sean, John mentioned Stevie's "**Isn't She Lovely**," the song written for his daughter Aisha. John even sang a line or two of "**Isn't She Lovely.**" One of many great songs on Stevie's 1976 album ***Songs in the Key of Life***, it's surprising to learn that "**Isn't She Lovely**" was never released as a single in the U.S. This was reportedly due to Stevie's refusal to edit the six-and-a-half-minute song down.

## HERB ALPERT
"Rise"

John was thinking about a including "Herb Albert horn solo" on **"Borrowed Time."** **"Borrowed Time"** was one of the tracks John had written in Bermuda during June and July. Although it was the second song recorded during the August *Double Fantasy* sessions, the reggae-inflected **"Borrowed Time"** didn't make the cut for the album, and the prospective horn solo was never recorded. The unfinished version was released on *Milk and Honey* in 1984.

In 1965 Alpert and the Tijuana Brass had a no. 7 *Billboard* hit with a sped-up instrumental version of **"A Taste of Honey,"** a song that the Beatles had recorded in a vocal version on their debut *Please Please Me* album two years earlier.

John was surely paying attention when Alpert's comeback instrumental **"Rise"** became a massive hit during the autumn of 1979. Alpert thus became the only artist to top the *Billboard* Hot 100 chart as both an instrumentalist and a vocalist, having sang on Bacharach and David's **"This Guy's in Love with You"** in 1968. John must have been heartened that one of his contemporaries was doing music that was both innovative and commercially successful.

Alpert sold a massive number of albums during the 1960s, reportedly even outselling the Beatles in the U.S. from the fall of 1965 until early 1967. An album cover like the one for *Whipped Cream and Other Delights* (Google it), on which **"A Taste of Honey"** was the first track, did nothing to hurt sales. Alpert recorded numerous Beatles covers through the years including "**All My Lovin'**," "**And I Love Her**," and "**Michelle**" in addition to less obvious choices such as "**Martha My Dear**." More recently, he recorded an instrumental version of John's "**Imagine**."

B.B. KING

"The Thrill Is Gone"

John referred the musicians to his own *Imagine* song "**How Do you Sleep**" and this King hit in suggesting the sound he wanted to achieve on "**I'm Losing You.**" John loved "**The Thrill Is Gone**" and had it on his home jukebox.

In a career that spanned over seven decades, "**The Thrill Is Gone**"— King's cover of a song originally released and co-written by Roy Hawkins in 1951—was the biggest hit record he ever had. Released on King's album *Completely Well*, it was a no. 15 *Billboard* Hot 100 hit in 1970 and rose to no. 3 on their R&B chart. It's a timeless track that showcases both King's stinging guitar licks and soulful vocals.

John owned a copy of King's classic album *Live at the Regal*, and there is a photo from 1965 of John and the Beatles with a copy of the album. The album contains classic versions of "**Every Day I Have the Blues**" and "**You Upset Me Baby**," among other songs.

King told a story about once reading an interview in which John stated that he'd "like to play guitar like B.B. King." King was heartened by the compliment and the pair later expressed their mutual admiration for each other during a phone call.

BUDDY HOLLY

"Listen to Me"

Next to his entry for "**Dear Yoko**," John refers to this Holly song and to
"**Dear Yoko**"'s precursor, "**Oh Yoko**," from his *Imagine* LP, in describ-
ing the general feel he wanted. For the guitar solo, he names Holly's
"**Listen to Me**." It's apparent John associated "**Dear Yoko**" with Holly.
He even sings like Holly on "**Dear Yoko**," with the "Well…a…hella…
hella" opening echoing Holly's "**Rave On**" vocal intro.

If you wanted to name one artist who had the most impact on John's
decision to pursue a musical career, Holly would be it. As great as Elvis
was, like almost all pop singers of the 1950s, he didn't write his own songs.
Holly wrote much his own material and thus provided a role model for
the burgeoning Lennon and McCartney songwriting team, a fact emphasized by Paul McCartney in the *Beatles Anthology* documentary. Holly's
Crickets even inspired John to come up with an insect-related play on
words when naming his band, the Beatles. As a rocker who wore glasses,
John had another thing in common with the young Texan.

John, George, and Paul each watched Buddy and the Crickets perform on the *Sunday Night at the London Palladium* TV show on March
2, 1958. John recalled watching Holly sing "**Peggy Sue**" that night:

"He was great! It was the first time I saw a Fender guitar. Being
played! While the singer sang!.. We did practically everything
he put out. … What he did with "3" chords made a songwriter

out of me. … He made it OK to wear glasses. I WAS Buddy Holly!"[95]

The first time John, Paul, and George laid down a song in a recording studio in July 1958, they chose Holly's hit "**That'll Be the Day.**" Indeed, this was the first song John actually learned to play on guitar (with his mom, Julia, using her banjo to assist him), and the first song John and Paul worked up together, with particular attention given to the vocal harmonies their combined voices created. (From their earliest days, the Beatles' vocal harmonies would always distinguish them from their competitors.) Around this time John composed his third song, the Holly-esque "**Hello Little Girl**." The song was good enough to be played during the Beatles' London Decca audition on New Year's Day, 1962.

The Beatles performed many of Holly's songs during their early days including "**Mailman, Bring Me No More Blues**" (also recorded during the *Get Back* sessions with John singing lead); "**Maybe Baby,**" which they also performed during the *Get Back* sessions; "**Crying, Waiting Hoping,**" which they recorded for their 1962 Decca audition; and "**Reminiscing,**" a December 1962 recording of which is preserved on the quasi bootleg album *Live at the Star Club Hamburg Germany.* John had Holly's covers of Chuck Berry's "**Brown Eyed Handsome Man**" and Little Richard's "**Slippin' and Slidin'**" on his Weybridge jukebox in the mid '60s. The Beatles recorded a faithful version of Holly's "**Words of Love**" for *Beatles for Sale* in 1964, while John later covered "**Peggy Sue**" on his *Rock and Roll* album.

---

95    Lewisohn

CHUCK BERRY
"Havana Moon"

John suggested his band of studio musicians listen to "**Havana Moon**" as he sought to describe the sound he desired for the chorus of "**I Don't Want to Face it**." John thought his demo recording was too fast in tempo and wanted them to take it slower. "**Havana Moon**" is not your typical Berry rocker. Rather, it's slow, sparse, and reflective. Berry's song was admittedly "inspired" by Nat King Cole's recording of "**Calypso Blues**," which Berry used to play in St. Louis nightclubs. Both "**Havana Moon**" and "**Calypso Blues**" are in the DNA of the Kingsmen's "**Louie Louie**," which was written by Richard Berry in the mid-1950s and released by the band in 1963.

"Havana Moon" was originally released as a B-side of Berry's 1956 single "**You Can't Catch Me**." That song loomed large in John's life as he used it as the basis for one of his most famous compositions, the Beatles' "**Come Together**." After describing in an interview that he'd come up with "**Come Together**" while jamming on Berry's "**You Can't Catch Me**," Berry's publisher sued John for plagiarism. The "flat top" line in "**Come Together**" was not helpful to his lawyers since it mimics a line in "**You Can't Catch Me**." The suit was settled years later with John agreeing to record several of the publisher's songs. Thus, John recorded "**You Can't Catch Me**" for his *Rock 'N Roll* album and the Lee Dorsey hit "**Ya Ya**" for *Walls and Bridges* to settle the case.

John had a 45 of Berry's 1964 hit "**No Particular Place to Go**" on his Weybridge jukebox.

As far as influences go, no other artist had a greater impact on the evolution of the Beatles music than Berry. The Beatles recorded no less than nine Berry songs in their career, two of which—**"Roll Over Beethoven"** and **"Rock and Roll Music"**—were on official releases, and seven of which were done at the BBC. John and Yoko chose Berry to be their musical guest when they co-hosted *The Mike Douglas Show* for a week in February 1972. Berry joined the pair and Elephant's Memory to perform "**Memphis**" and "**Johnny B. Goode.**"

CHRISTOPHER CROSS
"Sailing"

**"Sailing"** became the no. 1 song in the U.S. on August 30, 1980. *Double Fantasy* engineer Lee DeCarlo remembered John's fondness for the song:

> "He was very into Christopher Cross. He thought he was wonderful. John was into a very sailing mood in that time of his life. He had just sailed to Bermuda. I'm not sure what the song was, but he went 'I had this idea from listening to **'Sailing'** by Christopher Cross.'"[96]

John and a small crew had just sailed from Newport, Rhode Island, to Hamilton, Bermuda, in early June, so it's not surprising that he would be attracted to **"Sailing."** The week-long journey was a revitalizing experience that at one point saw John left on the deck by himself, steering the *Megan Jaye* sailboat through a severe storm. Recall that John had sailing in his blood via his father, Freddie, a merchant seaman. He also enjoyed reading about the adventure of ocean explorers like Thor Heyerdahl.

Remembering the profound experience steering the *Megan Jaye* to safety in his *Playboy* interview, John stated:

---

96   Sharp *Starting Over*

"Once I accepted the reality of the situation, something greater than me took over and all of a sudden I lost my fear. I actually began to enjoy the experience and I started to shout out old sea shanties in the face of the storm, screaming at the thundering sky."[97]

This was no joke. Crewmate Tyler Coneys remembered: "It was a huge storm and everyone thought we might die."[98] It's clear that the trip effected John in a profound way. It's significant that within days of arriving in Bermuda, a revitalized John had seemed to recapture his muse, writing new songs and revising old ones at a feverish pace. These "Bermuda tapes" were recorded on two Panasonic boomboxes (old-school "double-tracking" by playing along to a prerecorded tape while also recording live) purchased upon his arrival in Bermuda. Jack Douglas, who became the first outsider to hear these tapes—later recalled that John double tracked his singing due to his insecurity about his singing voice. These songs would comprise the core of John's contributions to **Double Fantasy** and **Milk and Honey.**

Cross' **"Sailing"** is quite peaceful and relaxing as it evokes a nautical trip on a placid waters. It really doesn't sound like any other song. John listening to the "soon I will be free" lines are quite poignant in light of the fate that soon awaited him.

**"Sailing"** is on Cross's 1980 debut album, **Christopher Cross,** which went on sell five million copies. The first single released from the album, **"Ride Like the Wind,"** stayed at no. 2 on the *Billboard* Singles chart for four weeks in April and May. It was kept out of the no. 1 spot by Blondie's **"Call Me,"** which was on the soundtrack of the popular Richard Gere

---

97    Sheff and Golson

98    *Bermuda Tapes* app

movie, *American Gigolo.*

"**Ride Like the Wind**" owed at least part of its success to the familiar, soulful vocals contributed by Michael McDonald of the Doobie Brothers. *Christopher Cross* also featured guest appearances by such rock luminaries as Don Henley of the Eagles, J.D. Souther, and Nicolette Larson.

Cross cleaned up at the Grammy Awards the following year when he won Best New Artist, Album of the Year, and Record and Song of the Year for "**Sailing**," which Cross composed himself. Cross' winning streak continued into the fall of 1980 when "**Never Be the Same**" rose to no. 15 on the *Billboard* chart, which is where it stood during last week of John's life. In 1981 Cross again hit no. 2 on the *Billboard* chart with "Arthur's Theme (Best That You Can Do)."

Although the hits stopped coming after another year or two, Cross is still a popular live attraction, often performing John's "**Imagine**" as his encore. In 2018 Cross affirmed his Beatles connection by touring in celebration of the 50th anniversary of the Beatles *White Album* as part of a band that included Todd Rundgren and Joey Molland of Badfinger.

To its credit (or blame), in the 21st century "**Sailing**" has retrospectively inspired its own genre of music, "yacht rock," decades after it was first released.

In a note dated June 11, 1980, that included a sketch depicting himself, the *Megan Jaye*, and the sun, John summed up what sailing meant to him when he made this inscription in the *Megan Jaye* logbook upon docking in Bermuda:

*There's no place like nowhere... Love, John*

ERIC TROYER

"Mirage"

Released in early 1980 on Chrysalis Records, "**Mirage**" is an exquisite slice of Beatle-y pop that should have been a bigger hit than it was, although it did get to no. 43 on Billboard's Adult Contemporary chart. Troyer wrote "**Mirage**," proving that he is a talented songwriter in addition to being a fine singer. Listening to "**Mirage**" you can see how Jack Douglas—who produced the track—believed that Troyer's voice and John's would complement each other perfectly.

In a correspondence with the author, Troyer wrote that he was all but certain that Douglas had played "**Mirage**" for John, along with other samples of his work, prior to his being hired to sing on *Double Fantasy*. When the pair met, John indicated to Eric that he was familiar with his singing.

Troyer worked extensively with John on the background vocals for "**Woman**." That "**Woman**" is arguably the strongest track on *Double Fantasy* is due in no small part to the way John's vocal blends with Troyer's. Prior to his death, John had selected "**Woman**" to be the second single released from *Double Fantasy*. It would go on to be a no. 1 hit in the U.K. and a no. 2 hit in the U.S. Due to its popularity and airplay, "**Woman**" is now likely the track from *Double Fantasy* that modern listeners are most familiar with. Troyer has said of "**Woman**": "It's Just a staggering song. It's so beautiful."[99]

---

99    Sharp *Starting Over*

Through the years Troyer has lent his voice to the recordings of a diverse group of artists including Kiss, Aerosmith, Billy Joel, Barbra Streisand, James Taylor, Carly Simon and Julian Lennon. Among the songs on which you've heard him sing are Celine Dion's "It's All Coming Back to Me Now"; Bonnie Tyler's "Total Eclipse of the Heart" and "Holding Out for a Hero" (Troyer has a long association with songwriter and producer Jim Steinman); and Billy Joel's "Tell Her About It" and "Uptown Girl." In 1988 he co-founded Electric Light Orchestra Part II (later renamed The Orchestra) with ex-ELO drummer Bev Bevan. They are still active today.

CHEAP TRICK

"I Want You to Want Me (Live)"

At the suggestion of Jack Douglas, their first producer, guitarist Rick Nielsen and drummer Bun E. Carlos of Cheap Trick were brought in to play on John's **"I'm Losing You"** and Yoko's **"I'm Moving On."**

In 2016, Nielsen explained how he and Carlos came to play on *Double Fantasy* to Howard Stern:

> "John was looking for a heavier sound because if you listen to *Double Fantasy* now it sounds kind of loungey to me and it sounds like studio guys, which it was. He wanted a harder edge."[100]

Successfully incorporating hard rock, pop, and new wave into their music, Cheap Trick were one of the most successful American bands of the late '70s. Nielsen had lived in England during the late '60s and was an unabashed Anglophile. Cheap Trick's memorable cover of The Move's obscure 1972 song **"California Man"** on their excellent 1978 album *Heaven Tonight* being but one example. Cheap Trick had begun work on their fifth studio album, *All Shook Up* in early 1980 with George Martin and Beatles engineer Geoff Emerick travelling to a snowy Rockford, Illinois, to begin pre-production work. Tracks were then laid down in the milder climes of Montserrat at Martin's AIR Studios. Jack Douglas

---

100    Howard Stern Show Sirius XM, 4/6/16

and Martin would later share a laugh about how they had swapped artists with each other.

According to Fred Seaman,[101] John had listened to some of Cheap Trick's albums before agreeing to Douglas's suggestion that they join the sessions. Upon listening, John noted a distinct Beatles influence in their music. Among the tracks John would have known by the band were their 1979 hit "**I Want You to Want Me,**" from their highly successful (#4, U.S.) ***Cheap Trick at Budokan*** album (for which Douglas supervised the mixing process); "**Dream Police,**" the title track of the (no. 6 U.S.) 1979 album of the same name; "**Taxman, Mr. Thief,**"[102] from their eponymous 1977 debut album, the only band album produced by Douglas; and "**Surrende**r," their best-known song excepting "**I Want You to Want Me.**" The Japanese connection might have piqued John's interest in the ***Budokan*** album. John spent his summers in Japan in the late '70s, and Cheap Trick was huge there.

John was likely aware of the band's current hit, "**Everything Works if You Let It,**" which was produced by George Martin and sounds like a lost Paul McCartney rocker. The song was recorded for the ***All Shook Up*** album but donated to the soundtrack of the movie *Roadie*. "**Everything Works if You Let It**" turned out to be better than anything else of the released album, and the song is underserving of its obscure status. A 45 of "**Everything Works if You Let It**" was included with the Cheap Trick four song EP (extended-play) ***Found All the Parts*** in June 1980. (The EP was part of Epic's short-lived NU Disk series of EPs.) Despite the fact that they were listed as having been recorded as far back as 1976, the ***Found All the Parts*** tracks were in fact produced as new studio recordings by Jack Douglas in late 1979. Considering that these were the first

---

101   Seaman

102   With its shout-out to former British PM Edward Heath, this song tips its hat to the Beatles' "**Taxman**," a fact that was likely noted by John.

recordings he'd produced for the band since 1976, logic would dictate that Douglas would have played the EP for John. The lead-off track, "**Such a Good Girl**," is a great song that, like "**Everything Works if You Let It**," doesn't deserve its obscure status.

During the session, Rick Nielsen informed John that Cheap Trick's "fake live" version of the Beatles' **Day Tripper** from *Found All the Parts* was a hit in Phoenix.[103]

Cheap Trick's cover of Fats Domino's was "**Ain't that a Shame**" from *Cheap Trick at Budokan* was clearly inspired by John's version recorded for his *Rock and Roll Album*. "**Ain't That a Shame**" was the first song John played on the banjo as a teenager, under the tutelage of his mother, Julia. John had met Fats when the Beatle played in New Orleans, but Apple Record's Tony King would later recall taking John to see Fats at the Flamingo Hotel in Las Vegas during the "Lost Weekend" era. When Fats said he was honored by John's presence John replied: "No. You're the man I've come to see. You shouldn't be honored to meet me. I should be honored to meet you."[104]

Rick Nielsen would affirm that John knew who the band was because when he walked into the Hit Factory John recognized Neilson (who had appropriated "Bowery Boy" Huntz Hall's distinctive look) from his photos and shouted "it's you" when he spotted him. This was although John didn't make the connection when told the names of the two members (Nielsen and drummer Bun E. Carlos) that were coming to play, but he knew the name Cheap Trick.

During their day at the Hit Factory Carlos and Nielsen played on John's "**I'm Losing You**" and Yoko's "**I'm Moving On**." Neither of their performances made the *Double Fantasy* album although their

---

103   Sharp *Starting Over*

104   *The Ballad of John and Yoko*

arrangements for both songs were reportedly imitated later by the studio musicians. The "**I'm Losing You**" take with Cheap Trick—thought to be superior to the album version by many fans—was finally released in 1998 on the *John Lennon Anthology*. Its hard rock arrangement may have been thought to be out of place amongst the mellower sounds on *Double Fantasy*. Their "**I'm Moving On**" take with Yoko has never been released.

Nielsen made this startling revelation during his Stern interview:

> "After we recorded, we were talking about doing another album with him. ...Cheap Trick being John Lennon's band."[105]

John backed by Cheap Trick. That would've been pretty cool!

Cheap Trick performed a touring 40th Anniversary tribute to *Sergeant Pepper's Lonely Hearts Club Band* along with guest vocalists in 2007. George Martin provided the band with the original orchestrations for accuracy and Geoff Emerick engineered the shows. Nielsen attended Martin's 2016 funeral.

Nielsen missed the birth of his son Dax on August 12, 1980, to go to New York to play with John. He recently recalled:

> "I always tell people that if it had been McCartney asking I would have been at the hospital. But it was John Lennon, the hero of heroes of millions of people, including me. I bought some Cuban cigars which were contraband in the United States at that time. And while we were recording—John, Yoko, Jack

---

105   Stern interview 4/6/16

JOHN LENNON : 1980 PLAYLIST

Douglas, myself—we smoked cigars as a toast to my son."[106]

Cheap Trick's **"Stop This Game"** was written up in the *Billboard's* "Top Single Picks" page in the November 8, 1980 issue. In the same issue *All Shook Up* was listed in the album "Spotlight" feature that prominently listed Martin's name as the album's producer.

The December 6, 1980 issue of *Billboard* was seen by John because, according to Fred Seaman, he had circled **"(Just Like) Starting Over"** and pointed an arrow indicating that it was going to no. 1. *Double Fantasy* was a new entry on the album chart at no. 25, one place behind Cheap Trick's *All Shook Up.*

Cheap Trick covered John's **"Gimme Some Truth"** in 2019.

---

106   Rick Nielsen on Sirius XM 7/5/20.

## MORRIS ALBERT
"Feelings"

No, it's not a misprint. Perhaps you're wondering what this schmaltz classic is doing in a book about one of rock and roll's foremost practitioners?

On the night of August 19, 1980, director Jay Dubin spent an evening filming the ***Double Fantasy*** recording sessions for the purpose of making a video for **"Starting Over."** He later reported that one of his assistants sang **"Feelings"** that night, with John joining in and supplying piano.[107] **"Feelings"** was a no. 6 Billboard hit for the Brazilian-born Albert in the fall of 1975, just as John had become a father again and was beginning his self-imposed retirement from recording and public life. **"Feelings"** stayed in the Billboard Hot 100 chart for an unusually long eight months, and this "familiarity breeds contempt" factor may have been what caused it to become scorned by many listeners.

**"Feelings"**[108] was widely mocked in the '70s and in subsequent years as insipid dreck. Just what exactly were these "Feelings" that Morris was going on about? He never really says! Along with ill-remembered 1970s top 40 staples like Debbie Boone's inescapable **"You Light Up My Life,"** the Captain & Tennille's insipid **"Muskrat Love,"** Bo Donaldson and the Heywoods guilty-pleasure **"Billy, Don't be a Hero,"** and Terry Jacks' nails-on-chalkboard **"Seasons in the Sun," "Feelings"** is often ranked high whenever "worst songs" lists are compiled.

---

107  Sharp *Starting Over*

108  Legendary New York deejay Dan Ingram used to call **"Feelings"** "the subway song." Get it?

Perhaps it was maturity or a sentimental streak that occasionally surfaced in his music (on beautiful songs like "**Goodnight**" and "**Grow Old with Me**"), but John might have actually dug "**Feelings.**" We know that he loved two only slightly less treacly songs—Barbra Streisand's "**The Way We Were**"[109] and Billy Joel's "**Just the Way You Are**"—so his fondness for (or at least tolerance of) "**Feelings**" might make sense. There's also a decent chance that John was goofing around and just singing whatever cheesy song came to mind at the time. Perhaps I should note that Fred Seaman later reported that John was on stronger stimulants than caffeine on this night.[110]

This would turn out to be the only video footage shot during the **Double Fantasy** sessions. Although the film footage wasn't used at the time—possibly due to John's dissatisfaction with his appearance—Dubin did manage to record and preserve John letting his hair down and rocking out. Perhaps more of the footage shot that night will surface one day? Wouldn't it be cool to watch John singing "**Feelings**"?

---

109    Elliot Mintz has described "**The Way We Were**" as Yoko's favorite song.

110    Seaman

# STUDIO JAM
## AUGUST 19, 1980

Aware of the sessions' historical import, producer Jack Douglas later revealed he was surreptitiously constantly recording John in the vocal booth at the Hit Factory from the outset of the ***Double Fantasy*** sessions. This would explain why on many of the unauthorized bootlegs of the sessions John can be clearly heard, while the band is distant and at a much lower volume. The "oldies jam" outlined below appears to have been sourced from the audio to Dubin's video which captures not only John's singing, but the band at full volume behind him. This tape has been in circulation among bootleggers for many years, and was popular with fans for its notable audio quality and because it revealed that the thirty-nine-year-old John still loved the rock and roll that he'd first turned him on as a teenager.

August 19 was a long day for John and the band. It began at noon and didn't end until three the following morning. With nothing else to do while the film lighting and cameras were being prepared, John and the band decided to jam to pass the time. The tape begins with versions of "**(Just Like) Starting Over**" (the "My mama done told me" line John sings at the start is from "**Blues in the Night**" which was popularized by Woody Herman and Dinah Shore[111] in the 1940s) and "**I'm Losing You.**" The video of John performing "**I'm Losing You**" was uploaded to YouTube a few years ago. That along with a brief snippet of Yoko and the

---

111    Dinah was still performing "**Blues in the Night**" in concert during the summer of 1980.

band performing **"I'm Moving On"** are the only pieces of Dubin's video to surface in the past forty years.

As for the audio, the songs are as follows:

BOBBY DARIN

"Dream Lover"

John has some fun messing around with Darin's lyrics singing that he desires a **"Dream Lover"** "so I don't have to sleep alone." Even so, John turns a very passionate vocal here and the band falls in nicely behind him. Listening, one is reminded of the voice that sang songs like **"Rock and Roll Music"** and **"Twist and Shout"** in the early days of the Beatles. That passionate voice is not very much in evidence on John's officially released 1980 recordings, but it comes through loud and clear on this version of **"Dream Lover."** John had recorded himself performing Darin's 1959 smash **"Beyond the Sea"** at home in the late 1970s, but his inspiration there seems to have been Charles Trenet's original version **"La Mer,"** as John speaks some half-baked French in attempting to imitate the Trenet recording.

Released in 1959, two years into a career that kicked off with **"Splish Splash,"** **"Dream Lover"** got to no. 2 on the *Billboard* Hot 100. The song showed Darin to be an excellent songwriter with a maturity beyond his years. This was confirmed months later with his no. 1 hit **"Mack the Knife,"** which showed the teen idol could give Frank Sinatra a run for his money. Sinatra gave a shout-out to the long departed Darin when he recorded Mack the Knife in the 1980s.

The Beatles performed two Darin-related songs during the 1969

*Get Back* sessions:[112] his 1958 song **"Queen of the Hop"**—a Top 10 hit on both sides of the Atlantic—and Darin's composition **"Early in the Morning,"** which was covered by Buddy Holly in 1958.

Without missing a beat, John begins to sing **"Stay."**

---

112  Sulpy

## MAURICE WILLIAMS AND THE ZODIACS
## "Stay"

Maurice Williams wrote **"Stay"** in 1953. The song was a no. 1 hit in the U.S. and a no. 14 hit in England late in 1960. This was a crucial time when the Beatles returned from their first trip to Germany and saw what has been described as the embryonic stages of Beatlemania at their first shows back home in Liverpool that December. The Beatles were soon performing "Stay" live, with John singing the lead.

**"Stay"** has been covered by the Hollies and the Four Seasons (both in 1964) and in a live version by Jackson Browne released in 1978 on his *Running on Empty* album. That version was widely played on the radio as was the one that Bruce Springsteen and the E Street Band performed (with Browne) on the 1979 *No Nukes* album, which documented the September 1979 concerts at Madison Square Garden. Although it's possible John was familiar the Browne and Springsteen recordings—both were regularly played on WNEW-FM in New York—he probably was thinking of Williams' oldie. John quickly shuts down the band's performance of **"Stay"** when he can't reach a high note saying "I'm a spoil sport. If I can't reach the note I have to stop."

## ELVIS PRESLEY
"Mystery Train"

Elvis's Sun Records recording of this Junior Parker song is surely part of rock's holy grail and not just because it helped put Elvis on the map. John and the band perform a surprisingly complete and competent version considering that this a jam, as John has fun throwing in some whoops and imitating Elvis. John made numerous allusions to Elvis during his 1980 interviews including noting that "**Hound Dog**" was Sean's favorite song.

It would be difficult to overstate the importance of Elvis in the Beatles' lives. In describing the cataclysmic effect of hearing "**Heartbreak Hotel**" for the first time in 1956, John later said: "My whole life changed from then on. I was just completely shaken by it."[113] Paul McCartney described Elvis' coming on the scene in the 1950s in messianic terms in *The Beatles Anthology*.

Stu Sutcliffe didn't sing much during his tenure as a Beatle, but his showcase was Elvis' "**Love Me Tender**." Although John stated that "Elvis died when he went into the Army" after The King died, it's worth noted that the young Beatles performed several of Elvis's post-Army songs on stage including "**Are You Lonesome Tonight?**," "**I Feel So Bad**," "**(Marie's the Name) His Latest Flame**," and "**Wooden Heart**."

However, by the time of his appearance on the U.K. *Juke Box Jury* show on June 22, 1963, John had gone sour on Elvis. Asked to rate The

---

113    Lewisohn

King's new disc *(You're the) Devil in Disguise* John said: "I don't like it. Somebody said today 'He sounds like Bing Crosby now' and he does. I don't like him anymore."

The Beatles jammed on several Elvis tunes during the January 1969 *Get Beck* sessions including **"I Got Stung," "Milk Cow Blues," "That's Alright Mama,"** and **"My Baby Left Me."**[114]

Nevertheless, John championed Elvis during the early and mid-1970s, a time when The King's career was clearly past its prime and being an Elvis fan was not exactly fashionable. John performed **"Hound Dog"** at the 1972 "One to One" benefit at Madison Square Garden and often wore an ELVIS button when seen in public including when he served as presenter at the 1975 Grammy Awards telecast.

John recorded a version of Elvis' **"You're So Square (Baby I Don't Care)"** at home during the late '70s. He also recorded a home version of an old song associated with Elvis, **"Just Because,"** but John changes it around after singing the first line. In fact, he sounds like he's using the old song as a spark to write a new song of his own.

**John** sang the opening line from Elvis's cover of Hank Snow's **"(Now and Then There's) A Fool Such as I"**—"Pardon me if I'm sentimental..." in greeting *New York Times* music writer Robert Palmer upon his arrival at the Dakota for an interview. In an earlier article on the *Double Fantasy* sessions, Palmer had used the term "sentimental" to describe John's new single **"(Just Like) Starting Over."** Palmer's feature story on John appeared in the *Times* Arts and Leisure section on November 9 under the somewhat depressing headline "John Lennon: Must Artists Self-Destruct?"

"Elvis Orbison" was the name John gave himself during the *Double Fantasy* sessions. Elvis's **"I Want You, I Need You, I Love You"** was

---

114   Sulpy

mentioned by John in describing "**(Just Like) Starting Over**" during the BBC interview. Drummer Andy Newmark would later state: "(John) does what was clearly an Elvis impersonation"[115] on "**(Just Like) Starting Over.**"

In a word association questionnaire that John filled out in 1976 for *Creem* Magazine (you remember the "Creem Dreem," don't you?) John uncharitably—if accurately—described The King as "fat." Hey, it wasn't for nothing that the "John" character in the Rutles "mockumentary"was named Ron Nasty.

---

115    Quote from the *Soul to Song* documentary on ***Double Fantasy***.

THE BEATLES
"She's a Woman"

Guitarist Hugh McCracken—who had played on Paul and Linda McCartney's *Ram* album in 1971—is apparently trying to push John into doing this McCartney-sung **"I Feel Fine"** B-side from 1964. John advises "Hughie" that he "doesn't go back to the '60s, I come from the '50s." Although John is seemingly kidding around with McCracken here, he is making a point that is important to understanding where he was coming from in recording *Double* Fantasy. John was reconnecting with his pre-fame and even pre-Beatles self, and wasn't interested in competing with himself or his old band. This is why "Elvis Orbison" continually pops up on his songs. John was letting himself be inspired by the artists that turned him on so long ago.

It's instructive that **"She's a Woman"** is the only song in this jam session that was released after 1960, and it's the only one John doesn't really want to play. The band starts up **"She's a Woman"** three times but John never manages to offer more than a line or two. Finally, he advises them to "stop playing that fucking thing!"

Because John wanted at least one player he'd worked with before on the album, John insisted that Douglas hire McCracken for the *Double Fantasy* sessions. He had previous played on John's 1971 single "**Happy Xmas (War is Over)**." On that occasion, John told McCracken that his work on *Ram* had been "an audition to get to me. He said you were all right."

Many years later McCracken contrasted the two Beatles:

"Like Paul, (John) was extremely intelligent and aware of what he wanted in the studio. But you'd never find two more diametrically opposed personalities. I was working on **Double Fantasy** at the time of his death. How long did it take me to recover from that night? I still haven't recovered.[116]

McCracken passed away in 2013.

116  "Hugh McCracken: Guitarist Who Worked for Lennon and McCartney,"*Independent*, April 18, 2013, https://www.independent.co.uk/news/obituaries/hugh-mccracken-guitarist-who-worked-for-lennon-and-mccartney-8579183.html

## LITTLE RICHARD
"Rip it Up"

This was familiar territory for John, seeing as he'd covered this song (in a medley with Richard's "**Ready Teddy**") on his ***Rock and Roll*** album, which also contains his version of Richard's "**Slippin' and Slidin'**." John had both Richard's and Buddy Holly's versions of "**Slippin' and Slidin'**" on his jukebox during the mid-'60s. Richard's had "Long Tall Sally" on the B-side. Also on the jukebox was Richard's "**Ooh! My Soul**" b/w "**True Fine Mama**."

John and the Beatles first met Richard back in the fall of 1962 when they shared bills with him in Liverpool and during a two-week run at the Star Club in Hamburg. Richard was impressed with the young band and later described himself as their "first American fan." No one put on a show like Little Richard, and the Beatles no doubt learned a thing or two about onstage presentation studying at the foot of the master.

The Beatles recorded and officially released Richard's "**Long Tall Sally**" (a song that had literally left John speechless upon hearing it as a teenager, it was also one of the songs Paul played for him on piano during an informal audition the day they met) and "**Hey Hey Hey Hey**" (in tandem with "**Kansas City**"). In addition, they recorded "**Lucille**" and "**Ooh My Soul**" for the BBC. All of their Little Richard covers feature Paul singing lead. Richard was a major influence on Paul's singing as evidenced in the Beatles' Richard homage "**I'm Down**," which was released as the B-side of "**Help**." Upon Richard's death in May 2020, both Paul and Ringo issued statements honoring him and his contributions to the development of the Beatles' music with Paul acknowledging "I owe a lot of what I do to Little Richard."

After telling Dubin that he doesn't need to see the video because "I know what I look like ... a fuckin bird" he tells the director "This is the only time we get to boogie. They never allow us." Critics who later found *Double Fantasy* to be a bit too polished would no doubt agree.

## BO DIDDLEY
### "I'm a Man"

A straight-on blues number here, which sets it apart from the lighter fare played this night. Itself a rewrite of Muddy Waters' Willie Dixon-penned hit 1954 hit "**Hoochie-Coochie Man**," Diddley's song was recorded in a rock style by the Yardbirds in 1965, a version notable for Jeff Beck's innovative guitar work. Note that Waters responded to Diddley's "**I'm a Man**" with his own song "**Mannish Boy**," which seemingly made reference to Diddley's youth.

"**Mannish Boy**" had seen something of a revival four years earlier when Waters performed it at The Band's[117] farewell "Last Waltz" concert in San Francisco on Thanksgiving night 1976. (Given John' interest in Bob Dylan and Ringo's appearance in the Martin Scorcese film documenting the show, it's unlikely that John missed *The Last Waltz* film.) Waters also recorded a powerful new version of "**Mannish Boy**" with guitarist-producer Johnny Winter for his ***Hard Again*** album, which was released in January 1977. In March 1977 the Rolling Stones performed a raunchy "**Mannish Boy**" at the El Mocambo Tavern in Toronto, a recording of which was released on their ***Love You Live*** album the following September. So, it's possible that John was referencing "**Mannish Boy**" in addition to, or instead of, "**I'm a Man**" during this jam. The songs are nearly interchangeable as they both vamp on one chord throughout. Sometime in or around 1978 John had recorded himself at the Dakota

---

117    John owned a copy of The Band's highly influential 1968 debut album *Music from Big Pink.*

singing **"I'm a Man"** while accompanying himself on acoustic guitar.

## GENE VINCENT
### "Be-Bop-A-Lula"

John had recorded this for the ***Rock and Roll*** album, and liked it enough to make it the lead-off track on that album. John would later recall that he was playing "**Be-Bop-A-Lula**" with his band, the Quarrymen, at a church fete in Liverpool on July 6, 1957, the day he met Paul McCartney. Serendipitous meeting, that! Appropriately enough, "**Be-Bop-A-Lula**" was the first record Paul ever bought. John later recalled that the opening "Well…" made his hair stand on end. While playing deejay at his London home in the fall of 1968 for writer Jonathan Cott[118], John professed his love for "**Be-Bop-A-Lula**" while playing a 45 of Vincent's 1956 rockabilly number "**Woman Love**." Both songs were on the jukebox John owned in the mid-1960s.

Vincent's 1959 versions of American Songbook standards "**Summertime**" and "**Over the Rainbow**" inspired the Beatles to include both songs in their early live act.

---

118    Jonathan Cott, *Days That I'll Remember: Spending Time With John Lennon and Yoko Ono* (New York: Doubleday, 2013)

EDDIE COCHRAN

"C'mon Everybody"

A very short version is played. John, his girlfriend (and future wife) Cynthia Powell, and Stu Sutcliffe all attended one of Cochran/Gene Vincent concerts at the Liverpool Empire in March 1960, so it's natural that a Cochran song would remind John of one of Vincent's. This pairing of "**Be-Bop-A-Lula**" into "**C'mon Everybody**" actually replicated a Beatles *Get Back* sessions jam that took place on January 7, 1969. On that occasion they played Vincent's "**Lotta Lovin'**" between the two songs.[119]

The 1960 Empire show was only weeks before Cochran's fatal car crash on the final night of a subsequent U.K. tour. In 1980 John was one of a fairly small universe of people that had a memory of seeing Cochran perform live. Recall that it was Paul McCartney's ability to play (and sing the lyrics of) Cochran's "**Twenty Flight Rock**" that convinced John to let him join his band, so Cochran had an indirect hand in the conception of The Beatles.

Cochran's version of Ray Charles' 1956 hit "**Hallelujah I Love Her So**" inspired the Beatles to begin playing the song live. A 1960 recording of the group rehearsing the song in Liverpool was included on *Anthology Volume 1* in 1995.

The Beatles first played "**C'mon Everybody**" on their 1960 tour of Scotland backing the unfortunately named singer Johnny Gentle. They also played it during the *Get Back* sessions in 1969. The Sex Pistols (with

---

119   Sulpy

Sid Vicious on lead vocals filling in for the recently departed Johnny Rotten) recorded "**C'mon Everybody**" and Cochran's "**Something Else**" for their album *The Great Rock and Roll Swindle*, which had been released in 1979. As we'll see, John was aware that Vicious was playing at Max's Kansas City in 1978, and "**C'mon Everybody**" and "**Something Else**" were among the songs the troubled Sid played there.

## THE ROLLING STONES
## "Emotional Rescue"

The title track from the Stones album released in June 1980, **Emotional Rescue** has a backing reminiscent of their 1978 hit "**Miss You**"[120]. When the *Double Fantasy* sessions commenced on August 2, *Emotional Rescue* was the #1 album in the U.S., a position it would maintain for six weeks. Given *Emotional Rescue's* less than stellar reputation among Stones fans, its chart success upon its release seems surprising today. Indeed, the Stones didn't play "**Emotional Rescue**" live until 2013, thirty-three years after its release! Part of the reason for that lapse is that the Stones didn't tour to support *Emotional Rescue* in 1980. By the time they hit the road for their 1981 U.S. tour, they had another hit album, *Tattoo You*, and hit single, "Start Me Up," to showcase. Jagger sings the better part of "**Emotional Rescue**" in a falsetto, something that did nothing to endear the song to the Stones largely male fan base. In addition, rumor has it that Keith Richards has never been too fond of "**Emotional Rescue.**"

Although John was often derisive towards Mick (whom he dismissed as a mere "company man"[121] in his September 1979 taped diary) and the Stones, his interviews reveal that he considered them—along with Bob Dylan—as the only worthy rivals to the Beatles. Even in 1980, it was still the Beatles vs. the Stones, with both Lennon, McCartney, and the Stones

---

120  Readers of this author's book *Sounds Like Teen Spirit: Stolen Melodies, Ripped-off Riffs, and the Secret History of Rock and Roll* (2016 Edition) will recall that John thought Mick and Keith had nicked the melody from his *Wall and Bridges* track "Bless You" for "Miss You."

121  A category in which he also included Messrs. Dylan, and McCartney.

hitting the top of the U.S. charts in competition with one another. John and Mick hung out together during the '70s. While in L.A. in early 1974 John produced Mick singing a cover of Willie Dixon's **Too Many Cooks (Spoil the Soup)** that's pretty great. (It didn't see the light of day until it was released on *The Very Best of Mick Jagger* album in 2007.) May Pang wrote about her and John staying at Mick and Bianca Jagger's house in the Hamptons in the fall of 1974, and Mick was photographed attending the circus (of all things!) with John, Yoko, and Sean at Madison Square Garden in March 1977.

Fred Seaman later wrote that John cranked up the car radio and screamed with joy when the Stones' **"Miss You"** came on during a spring 1980 drive.

In his 2007 autobiography *Ronnie*,[122] Stones guitarist Ron Wood recounts an incident in which he alleges John once snorted heroin with the Stones while visiting them at their suite in the Plaza Hotel in New York. Woody writes that they later proceeded to the Atlantic Records studios where the Stones had been recording. Woody claims that once there, John joined the band as they jammed "a songbook of early soul and early Beatles catalogue" before John passed out due to the effects of the "gauge." Woody also writes that the session was recorded and speculates that the tape still exists in the Atlantic vault!

Not surprisingly, Woody is somewhat foggy as to the date of this incident. He seems to indicate it took place subsequent to the Stones appearance on *Saturday Night Live* on October 7, 1978, but it may have been some months earlier. On the show, which was hosted by then New York Mayor Ed Koch and marked the season premiere of *SNL's* fourth year, the Stones performed the *Some Girls* tracks **"Beast of Burden,"** **"Respectable,"** and **"Shattered."**

---

122   Ronnie Wood, *Ronnie* (London: MacMillan, 2007)

It's worth noting that Paul and Linda McCartney were photographed hanging out with Woody and his bandmates backstage prior to the Stones gig at the Palladium in New York on June 19, 1978. So the Stones were maintaining warm relations with both John and Paul.

Mick later stated that even though he lived nearby, he didn't see much of John in later years because he was considered to be among the "bad influences." Given Woody's story, this shouldn't shock anyone.

The *Emotional Rescue* track "**She's So Cold**" was on the U.S. charts in the fall of 1980.

During a photo and video shoot for the song "**Woman**" on November 26, John vetoed photographer Ethan Russell's suggestion that John lip sync to the song saying "I don't know ... I don't want to be like Mick, you know, prancing about at forty.[123]

In his December 1980 interview with Jonathan Cott, John brought up Jagger in the context of defending artists against the changing attitudes of the public and critics:

> "Take Mick, for instance. Mick's put out constantly good work for twenty years, and will they ever give him a break? Will they ever say, 'Look at him, he's number one, he's thirty-six, and he's put out a beautiful song, '**Emotional Rescue**,' it's up there'? I enjoyed it. Lots of people enjoyed it. So it goes up and down."[124]

It's instructive that John was wearing an old T-shirt with Mick's face on it when speaking these words.

---

123  Ethan Russell, *An American Story* (Ethan Russell & Associates, 2012)

124  Jonathan Cott, *Back to a Shadow in the Night: Music Writings and Interviews 1968-2001* (New York: Hal Leonard, 2002)

FUN FACT: ***Double Fantasy*** keyboardist George Small later told author Ken Sharp that the guitar lick that connects the end of John's **"I'm Losing You"** to Yoko's **"I'm Moving On"** on ***Double Fantasy*** was "quoting from" **"Miss You."**[125]

---

125   Sharp, *Starting Over*

## NOEL COWARD

"Matelot"

Things were hectic at the Dakota as John and Yoko were preparing to rehearse their new songs with the session musicians for the first time. Amid the hubbub Fred Seaman found John "Engrossed in a Noel Coward record." "Listen ... he's crying!" John said to Yoko.[126]

This song, though not named, is likely "**Matelot**,"[127] Coward's plaintive ballad of a young French sailor. It *does* sound like Coward is nearly crying at certain points in the song. The song was personal for Coward since he wrote it for actor Graham Payn, who would go on to be his companion for over thirty years. Payn sang "**Matelot**" in a 1945 London production of Coward's musical *Sigh No More*. Coward often performed "**Matelot**" in his nightclub act in later years and it's included on his popular *Noel Coward at Las Vegas* album, which he recorded at the Desert Inn there in 1955.

Coward has been described as England's first pop star. You could put his photo next to the word "urbane" in the dictionary. He was the only Englishman composing for the theater widely thought to be in the same league with the great American composers of the era like Irving Berlin and Cole Porter.

Although they were from distinctly different eras, John and Coward

---

126   Seaman

127   Though hardly a Coward expert, the author did consult with three internationally prominent Coward devotees before making this judgment. Runner-ups to "**Matelot**" were "**20th Century Blues**" and "**If Love Were All**."

had quite a lot in common. Both men were known for their acid wit and clever wordplay. Like John, Coward wore many creative hats: singer; writer (his works include the story and screenplay for the classic romantic 1945 film drama, *Brief Encounter*); film actor (his last role was his memorable turn as crime boss in *The Italian Job* in 1969); playwright (*Private Lives, Blythe Spirit*); live performer (he was a familiar presence to television audiences of the 1950s and '60s, and he also had a cabaret act); and songwriter (**"Mad Dogs and Englishmen," "Someday I'll Find You,"** and **"I'll See You Again,"** to name just a few).

John's unreleased song from around 1976, **"She's a Friend of Dorothy"** (a phrase referencing Judy Garland's role in *The Wizard of Oz* that was once used as code to indicate someone was gay) has a distinct Coward vibe. John put considerable work into the song, recording seven takes at home. The song has a more uplifting melody than his other compositions from that time.

Unfortunately, John's admiration for Coward was not reciprocated. After meeting John and Paul at a party in 1964 Coward told a reporter: (They) seemed like nice, pleasant young men.... Of course, they are totally devoid of talent."[128]

The Beatles heard about this rare putdown from the Great Man and Ringo later related how they got their revenge:

"Noel Coward put his foot in us with that 'no talent' remark. We got him back later, when Brian (Epstein) came to us and said 'Noel Coward is downstairs and he wants to say "hi"—

128 Molly Driscoll, "'Hello, Goodbye, Hello': 6 Oddball Meetings between Celebrities," *The Christian Science Monitor*, August 6, 2012, https://www.csmonitor.com/Books/2012/0806/Hello-Goodbye-Hello-6-oddball-meetings-between-celebrities/Paul-McCartney-and-Noel-Coward

'Fuck off!' We wouldn't see him. I mean. "Sod off, Noel."[129]

After attending a Beatles concert in Rome the following year, Coward wrote:

> "The noise was deafening throughout and I couldn't hear a note they sang or a word they played, just one long, ear-splitting din. … Personally I should have liked to take some of those squealing young maniacs and cracked their heads together. … To realize the majority of the modern adolescent world goes ritualistically mad over those four innocuous, rather silly looking young men is a disturbing thought. Perhaps we are whirling more swiftly into extinction than we know."[130]

Let's hope Sir Noel was wrong about that one. I wonder what he would have thought of the state of the world in 2020 and beyond?

Coward's often world-weary outlook makes his songs appealing to contemporary audiences. For instance, Marianne Faithfull has performed Coward's "**20th Century Blues**" for years and it served as the title track of her 1996 album. Paul McCartney recorded Coward's "**A Room with a View**" for the Coward tribute album *Twentieth Century Blues: The Songs of Noel Coward*, which was curated by Neil Tennant of the Pet Shop Boys. Paul's "A Room with a View" wouldn't seem out of place with Beatle tracks like "**Martha My Dear**" and "**When I'm 64.**"

With John listening to an almost 40-year-old song in 1980, we see that he appreciated music beyond rock and roll and R&B, and that, again, the music of his youth was still relevant to him.

---

129   *The Beatles Anthology*

130   Graham Payn and Sheridan Morley, Editors. *The Noel Coward Diaries* (Boston: Little, Brown and Co., 1982)

## OLIVIA NEWTON-JOHN
"Magic"

## E.L.O.
"All Over the World"

In his September *Newsweek* interview, John cited these two current hit songs as examples of contemporary pop songs that he enjoyed. Asked why he had made a "commercial album" with **Double Fantasy**, John responded:

> "Because I love commercial music!...I like pop records. I like Olivia Newton-John singing "**Magic**" and Donna Summer singing whatever the hell she'll be singing. I like ELO singing "**All Over the World**." I can dissect it and criticize it with any critic in the business. ... But without any thought I *enjoy* it. I just enjoy it! That's the kind of music I like to hear."[131]

Both songs were from the movie *Xanadu*, a musical fantasy involving a roller disco that starred Newton-John along with Gene Kelly, in his final film role. Despite the fact that the movie was a box office disappointment, the soundtrack album to **Xanadu** was a worldwide success, and went double platinum in the U.S. Olivia and ELO also collaborated

---

131    Barbara Graustark, Vic Garbarini, and Brian Cullman, *Strawberry Fields Forever: John Lennon Remembered* (New York: Delilah, 1980)

on the Jeff Lynne-penned title track "**Xanadu**," which was a #1 single in the U.K. Olivia's duet with Cliff Richard, "**Suddenly**," was a top 20 hit in both the U.S. and the U.K. later in the year.

While John and Yoko were recording *Double Fantasy*, "**Magic**" was the U.S. *Billboard* # 1 single for four weeks in August 1980. "**Magic**" was written and produced by Olivia's long-time producer, John Farrar. Strangely enough, it was John who called out Olivia and Farrar's names in announcing that their recording of "**I Honestly Love You**" had won Record of the Year at the 1975 Grammy Awards. (In their absence the award was accepted for them by … Art Garfunkel. Well, why not?) "**Magic**" was Olivia's biggest U.S. hit to date, and was the third most-popular song in the U.S. in 1980, finishing behind only Pink Floyd's "**Another Brick in the Wall**" and Blondie's "**Call Me**." Olivia outdid herself in 1981 when the rather grating and insipid "Physical" spent a mind-boggling ten weeks atop the U.S. Hot 100.

A shimmering piece of pop rock, "**All Over the World**" still sounds great forty years later. It's no wonder John liked it! It was preceded by "**I'm Alive**," the first single ELO released from *Xanadu*—and a top 20 U.S. hit after its release in May. John was always complimentary toward ELO, calling them "son of Beatles" in a 1974 radio interview. Lynne produced George Harrison's 1997 album *Cloud Nine* and the duo formed the Traveling Wilburys supergroup with Bob Dylan, Tom Petty, and Roy Orbison the following year.

In a strange way, you might say that Jeff Lynne went on to work with John. In 1994 he was tasked by the three surviving Beatles (largely at George's insistence) with producing their overdubs onto John's home recordings of the songs "**Free as a Bird**" and "**Real Love**." These recordings were released on the Beatles' *Anthology Volume 1* and *Anthology Volume 2* respectively. Although some thought the songs ended up sounding a bit too much like ELO, Lynne did a reasonably good job under the circumstances. "**Real Love**"—which John came close to recording for ***Double Fantasy***—being a particular gem. Paul McCartney later revealed that the "Threetles" also began working with a tape of John's song "**Now and Then**" recorded in 1978. The work ceased when George Harrison (correctly) questioned whether the song was up to scratch quality-wise. Even so, Paul has said he may yet return to the studio to finish the recording with Lynne.

Lynne produced Ringo's cover of the Beatles song "I Call Your Name" in 1990. Two years later he produced three tracks on Ringo's *Time Takes Time* album. He went on to produce eight songs on Paul McCartney's 1997 album *Flaming Pie*, which was widely cited as Paul's best offering in years. Lynne later worked with George and his son Dhani on the production of George's excellent final album, the posthumously released *Brainwashed*. Dhani opened Jeff Lynne's ELO shows in 2019. Given these myriad Beatle connections and John's admiration for his music, it's tempting to suppose that if he had lived John would have collaborated with Lynne in some fashion.

As for the film *Xanadu*, the less said the better. To its credit it did help inspire the creation of the Golden Raspberry Awards, which annually recognize the very worst in filmmaking. *Xanadu* became a Broadway musical in 2007. With the addition of several other ELO and Newton-John hits to the *Xanadu* songs, the show proved a success and ran for over a year on Broadway. Live productions of the musical have continued to be presented around the world in the years since. As ever, the music from *Xanadu* is hard to resist, and still holds up well forty years on.

KATE BUSH
"Babooshka"

John asked Fred Seaman to procure a 45 of "**Babooshka**" for him at the outset of the ***Double Fantasy*** sessions.[132] This might have been because he wanted to play it for the musicians as an example of a certain type of sound he was hoping to achieve during the sessions, or maybe he just liked the song. This, of course, was in the prehistoric age when you had to buy a physical copy of a song (or tape it) if you wanted to hear it.

Kate Bush is a unique artist who defies conventional classifications. An avid reader of *Billboard*, John may have become aware of "**Babooshka**" by perusing the British charts contained therein. Another possibility is that John might have heard the song on WNEW-FM, where his friend Scott Muni featured a "Things from England" segment every Friday afternoon on his show. In it, Muni would sample whatever songs were topping the charts in the U.K., without regard as to whether the songs fit the station's album rock format.

Bush made her first (and to date, only) appearance on a U.S. variety show when she appeared on *Saturday Night Live* on December 9, 1978. The guest host that week was Monty Python's Eric Idle, who was fresh off his triumph spoofing the Beatles in his *All You Need is Cash* "Rutles" mockumentary, so it's likely that John was watching that

---

132   Seaman

night. Bush performed a song she had written when she was fourteen, **"The Man with the Child in His Eyes"** (sitting on a piano played by a pre-Letterman Paul Shaffer) and **"Them Heavy People."** The former song was Bush's follow-up to her astonishing debut single **"Wuthering Heights,"** a no. 1 hit in the U.K. for a month starting in March of 1978 and surely a song that John would have been familiar with. A tribute to novelist Emily Bronte, with whom Bush shared a birthday, **"Wuthering Heights"** marked the first time a female artist in the U.K. and solely written and performed a no. 1 hit. And Bush was only nineteen at the time! **"The Man with the Child in His Eyes"** was the first Bush song to crack the U.S. top 100, peaking at no. 85 in early 1979.

Bush adds a haunting vocal refrain to Peter Gabriel's **Games Without Frontiers**, an anti-war song released as a single in early 1980 and included on Gabriel's **third self-titled album**, which was released in May. **Games Without Frontiers** was widely heard on U.S. FM radio (including WNEW-FM in New York) and made it to no. 4 in the U.K., making it Gabriel's highest charting single there to date. If you were wondering just what Bush is singing throughout the song it turns out it's "Jeux sans frontiers," the French translation of the title.[133]

In spite of her worldwide popularity, Bush has achieved only one top 40 hit in the U.S., "Running Up that Hill," and one gold album, *The Sensual World*, over the course of her forty-plus year career.

Lyrically, **"Babooshka"** is about a woman wearing a disguise to test her lover's fidelity. It rose to #5 on the U.K. chart. The album that contained **"Babooshka,"** *Never For Ever*, went gold in the U.K. and made Bush the first female artist ever to have a No. 1 album in the U.K. It is a testament to John's open-mindedness as an artist that he liked and respected the work of a female artist half his age.

---

133   https://americansongwriter.com/
games-without-frontiers-peter-gabriel-behind-the-song/

The appreciation was mutual. A clip has surfaced of a 17-year-old Kate performing the Beatles' **"Come Together"** with her band at a pub in 1977. In 1981 she purchased a statue of John and Yoko in their "Two Virgins" pose at an auction house.

## DAVID BOWIE
"Ashes to Ashes"

Upon watching Bowie's strikingly innovative "**Ashes to Ashes**" video in the summer of 1980, John said "This is what I should be doing."[134] The song was a sequel to Bowie's breakthrough hit from a decade earlier, "**Space Oddity**," but this time "Major Tom's a junkie." A uniquely inventive song that didn't sound like anything else at the time, "**Ashes to Ashes**" was a huge success in the U.K., staying atop the singles chart for two weeks in late August and early September.

By the time he heard "**Ashes to Ashes**" John had hired former Bowie sideman Earl Slick to play guitar on *Double Fantasy*. In its way, hiring one of his sidemen was the highest possible compliment John could have given Bowie. John told the BBC[135] that Slick had worked with Bowie during his "mid-seventies...R&B incarnation." John noted that he didn't recall meeting Slick during the sessions for Bowie's *Young Americans*, although they both contributed to the album. In addition to "**Fame**," John plays guitar and sings on Bowie's *Young Americans* cover of "**Across the Universe**," a song of John's that he thought was not properly recorded when the Beatles tackled it in early 1968. Bowie's version isn't likely to make you forget the original.

John was said to watch *The Tonight Show* with Johnny Carson every night. Bowie appeared on the September 5, 1980 broadcast performing "**Ashes to Ashes**" and the classic *Hunky Dory* track "**Life on Mars**."

---

134   Seaman

135   Lennon, Ono,Peebles

This marked the only time Bowie performed "**Ashes to Ashes**" in public during 1980. The show was noteworthy because it featured Richard Pryor, who was making his first public appearance after a horrific accident in which set himself on fire while freebasing cocaine in June. This was also one of the final 90-minute *Tonight Show*s, which switched to an hour format permanently on September 17.

It's worth remembering that rock artists were rarely featured on *The Tonight Show* in 1980, so Bowie's appearance was something of an anomaly. Johnny's musical guests in 1980 included old school singers like Johnny Mathis, Pat Boone, and Robert Goulet along with country acts such as Tammy Wynette and Crystal Gayle. On this night, Bowie was greeted with effusive praise from Carson and loud cheers from the audience, many of whom seem to be fans of his. Bowie's rendition of "**Ashes to Ashes**" is unusual to hear because it doesn't feature any of the studio effects used on the album version. Rather the guitars of Carlos Alomar (who co-wrote "**Fame**" with John and Bowie) and G.E. Smith are to the fore. Bowie wore a red jacket as part of an outfit that—intentionally—copied James Dean's look in the 1955 film *Rebel Without a Cause*. In addition, Bowie's hair is styled to look like Dean's.

The video for "**Ashes to Ashes**" that so impressed John was directed by David Mallet. The video used the new Paintbox technique to stunning effect as it depicted Bowie dressed as a clown strolling on a beach holding a television with the image of a bulldozer approaching him from the rear. With the birth of MTV still almost a year away from changing the way pop music was marketed, Bowie had grasped the seemingly limitless artistic possibilities of marrying pop songs with video. Here, he was building on his pioneering "**Boys Keep Swinging**" video from the previous year.

The band that appeared on *The Tonight Show* also appears in the video for "**Fashion**," which was shot at the Hurrah club in New York that fall, and again directed by Mallet. Making a cameo in the video is May Pang, who later married Bowie's producer, Tony Visconti. (Funny how so many things tie in to each other, isn't it?) Mallet's videos for "**Ashes to Ashes**" and "**Fashion**" were voted the best videos of 1980 by the readers of the U.K.'s *Record Mirror*.[136] "**Fashion**" is an inventive song—its middle eight was likely inspired by the Boomtown Rats' song "**Rat Trap**"—that features Robert Fripp's distinctive guitar work.

Bowie was justifiably proud of "**Ashes to Ashes**," calling it "certainly one of the better songs I've ever written." Some Bowiephiles would, in retrospect, see the song—and the album it was on, *Scary Monsters and Super Creeps*—as marking the end of Bowie's decade-plus run of brilliant work. The later years of the 1980s would see his output take a decidedly hit-or-miss turn with forays into dance rock (the highly successful *Let's Dance*), noise rock (two Tin Machine albums) and mediocre records like *Tonight* and *Never Let Me Down*. Not coincidentally, Bowie didn't work with long-time producer Tony Visconti in the two decades following the release of *Scary Monsters*.

Bowie said that "**Ashes to Ashes**"—and a number of his other songs— were inspired by actor Danny Kaye's singing the song **"Inchworm"** in the 1952 movie *Hans Christian Anderson*. "There's something so sad and mournful and poignant about it," Bowie later said.[137]

Roy Bittan of Bruce Springsteen's E Street Band plays piano on "**Ashes to Ashes**." One of rock's most underrated players, Bittan had previous lent his talents to Bowie's *Station to Station*. Fortuitously, Bittan was recording what would become *The River* during protracted sessions with Springsteen at New York's Power Station in early 1980 while Bowie

---

136   Pegg, *The Complete David Bowie*

137   *American Songwriter* interview, 2003.

was working on "**Scary Monsters**" down the hall at the same studio.

John spoke fondly of Bowie—his sometime traveling companion—in his December BBC interview. He recalled being impressed watching Bowie make up the song "**Fame**" in the studio in January 1975, and described his own contributions to the song which earned him a co-writing credit on Bowie's first no. 1 hit in the U.S. John went on to say that he "loved" "**Fame**" and called Bowie "an amazing guy."

"I must say I admire him for the vast repertoire of talent he has. ... I was never around when the Ziggy Stardust thing came, because I'd already left England while all that was going on, so I never really knew what he was. And meeting him doesn't give you much more of a clue ... but we seemed to have some kind of communication together, and I think he's great. The fact that he can just walk into that (Bowie stepped into the lead role of John Merrick in *The Elephant Man* and was starring in the show on Broadway as John spoke in December) and do that. I could never do that."[138]

John reportedly had plans to see Bowie in Bernard Pomerance's play *The Elephant Man* when he was killed. Bowie had taken on the challenging lead role of a real-life nineteenth century Englishman, Joseph "John" Merrick, who suffered from severe physical deformities. The play is especially challenging for the actor playing Merrick because he is not made up to reflect Merrick's appearance, but rather must convey Merrick's deformities with only his own speech and mannerisms. Having always been a theatrical live performer, Bowie's transition to the stage was a natural progression for him. By most accounts, Bowie gave a stunning performance as Merrick, enchanting New York theater critics when he made his Broadway debut (after performing with the road company in Denver and Chicago) on September 23 at the Booth Theater.

---

138   Lennon, Ono, Peebles

Shaken by John's assassination, Bowie cancelled a European tour that he had been planned for early 1981.

*Double Fantasy* guitarist Earl Slick returned to work with Bowie on his late career albums *Reality* (2003) and *The Next Day* (2013). With his determination to constantly be pushing new boundaries with each successive album, Bowie was perhaps the foremost embodiment of the Beatles' artistic legacy. He remained close to Yoko and Sean in later years prior to his death in January 2016.

Bowie later revealed that John had been the one to introduce him to *The Uncle Floyd Show*, a live, low budget television comedy show broadcast out of New Jersey on a UHF[139] channel. Bowie came to love the show and its characters, which were both the brainchild of "Uncle Floyd" Vivino. He later wrote the song "Sail Away" about the characters on the show. Fans of the show formed a special bond as if they shared a secret. **"Deep in the Heart of Jersey"** (an amusing re-write of **"Deep in the Heart of Texas"**) was the show's theme song.

---

139   Ask your parents.

WENDY CARLOS
"Sonic Seasonings"

A hard to classify album originally released in 1972, *Sonic Seasonings* consists of soundscapes mixed with music. It is generally considered to be a groundbreaking work and is often cited as the first "ambient" album, although that term was not yet in use in 1972. Drawing inspiration from Vivaldi's **"The Four Seasons,"** *Sonic Seasonings* was originally a two-record set with each of the four sides devoted to one of the seasons of the year. It the parlance of the day *Sonic Seasonings* was a "mind blower."

According to Albert Goldman's biography,[140] John was fascinated with *Sonic Seasonings*. Perhaps inspired by *Sonic Seasonings*, John inserted a couple of field recordings of his own on *Double Fantasy*. These included:

- A Japanese wishing bell rung three times to introduce the album prior to **"Starting Over."** This was a more optimistic echo of the ominous church bell sound at start of the 1970 *Plastic Ono Band* album. It was also a subtle reminder that John considered all of his artistic output to be of one piece.

- The ambient sounds of an airport terminal, including flight information being announced, on the outro of **"Starting Over."**

---

140    Albert Goldman, *The Lives of John Lennon* (New York: Morrow, 1988)

- Telegraph and busy signal sounds at the end of "**I'm Losing You**" (underscoring the "can't even get you on the telephone lyric"), segueing into Yoko's "**I'm Moving On.**" Jack Douglas later said these telegraph sounds are spelling out "I Love You, Yoko," a secret message that had been inserted at John's insistence.

- The sounds of the ocean and a ship's bell at the beginning and the end of "**Beautiful Boy.**"

- At the end of "**Watching the Wheels**" there are sounds that remind one of an amusement park followed by the sounds of footsteps. John had told Jack Douglas that he wanted the song to sound "circular," so this might have been their attempt at achieving that.

- There is the murmuring of a crowd at the beginning of Yoko's "**Yes, I'm Your Angel.**" This may have been inspired by John Cage's avant-garde ambient exercise "**4'33''**", to which they once paid tribute to on "**Two Minutes Silence**" from their 1969 album *Unfinished Music No. 2: Life With the Lions.*

Of course, John was no stranger to sound experiments as evidenced by his dropping a random AM radio broadcast of Shakespeare's *King Lear* into the mix of "**I Am the Walrus**," the *White Album* audio collage "**Revolution 9**," and his early albums with Yoko like *Two Virgins*, *Life with the Lions*, and the *Wedding Album*.

The Beatles' "**Carnival of Light**," a precursor to "**Revolution 9**" that the Beatles recorded at Paul McCartney's instigation in January 1967, remains unreleased. The over thirteen-minute recording has been described as less a song than a series of musical textures along the lines of

**"The Return of the Son of Monster Magnet"** on Frank Zappa and the Mothers of Invention's *Freak Out* album.

John's friend Elliot Mintz later recalled that he and John would exchange audio cassettes of "found sounds"—such as the noise of the traffic outside the Dakota—mixed with bits of music of John's own or from over the radio. John called these tapes "Mind Movies."

Sometime in 1967 John was photographed with a copy of *Electronic Music*, a various artist sampler that included two Carlos pieces: **"Variations for Flute and Electronic Sound"** and **"Dialogues for Piano and Two Loudspeakers."**

Carlos broke on the music in a big way in 1968 with the release of the wildly popular *Switched-On Bach* album, on which Carlos showcased the newly invented Moog synthesizer to great effect. Carlos was instrumental in the development of the new instrument, offering practical advice to inventor Robert Moog starting in 1966 as they went through the trial and error of perfecting the "Moog." You might say that Moog was the computer genius and Carlos the artist genius.

*Switched-On Bach* stands as a landmark album that introduced the synthesizer to the world, allowing musicians to access a new world of sounds on their recordings, and eventually spawning new genres of music including prog rock and techno. Later versions of the Moog synthesizer were heard on innovative recordings in the 1970s including Kraftwerk's **"Autobahn"** and Donna Summer's **"I Feel Love."**

Carlos next began a collaboration which resulted in her composing music for *A Clockwork Orange* and later, *The Shining*. She underwent gender reassignment surgery in the early 1970s, and took the new name Wendy Carlos.

In addition to being a great "headphone album" recorded in quadraphonic sound, *Sonic Seasonings* seeks to evoke the seasons using sounds like rain and thunder, ocean waves, and other field recordings. In the liner notes to **Sonic Seasonings** Carlos' collaborator Rachel Elkind describes their work as "psycho acoustics ... the manner in which the ear and brain react to sounds."

# YOKO'S SONGS

Since he was a teenager, John had fantasized about one day marrying a female artist. In his own eyes John was an artist first, even before he was a Beatle. Yoko's playful, interactive, and challenging conceptual art intrigued him in a way that nothing else could. Despite what anyone else thought, John loved her both as a woman and as an artist. He would spend the final days of his life focused on gaining her the recognition as an artist he had long thought she deserved.

John was passionate with regard to Yoko in their *Playboy* interview:

> "Anybody who claims to have some interest in me as an individual artist, or even as part of the Beatles, has absolutely misunderstood everything I've ever said if they can't see why I'm with Yoko. Any if they can't see that, they don't see anything."[141]

The following songs are ones that Yoko wrote while John was still alive with which he would have been familiar. This list excludes Yoko's **Double Fantasy** songs.

---

141   Sheff and Golson

## "DON'T BE SCARED"

A recording has surfaced of a 1980 rehearsal of this reggae style number with John on guitar. Yoko later recorded the song again for her *Season of Glass* album in early 1981.

## "NOBODY SEES ME LIKE YOU DO"

One of Yoko's best songs, it was rehearsed with the **Double Fantasy** band with John on guitar —plus some humorous commentary—in 1980. Yoko later stated[142] that "**Nobody Sees Me Like You Do**" "Could have been on **Double Fantasy**," and that John "Loved the chord sequence." A new version was recorded for Yoko's *Season of Glass* and released as a single in 1981. Roseanne Cash recorded an excellent version for the 1984 Yoko tribute album *Every Man Has a Woman*, which was released in 1984.

## "GOODBYE SADNESS"

Yoko recalled writing this song after visiting John in L.A. during their "Lost Weekend" separation. She remembered that John was not in good shape and she had been summoned to try to talk some sense into him. She wrote this on her flight back to New York.

## "MIND WEAVER"

Written while John was still alive under its original title, "**Mindfucker**." It was renamed and released on *Season of Glass* in 1981.

---

142 *Yoko Ono: A Spoken-word Discography* by Gillian G. Gaar, reprinted in *Goldmine Magazine* The Beatles Digest.

### "MOTHER OF THE UNIVERSE"

Yoko recalled playing this song on piano for John. It was later recorded for *Season of Glass*.

### "SILVER HORSE""

Yoko has said: "John loved that song. We were going to put it (on *Double Fantasy*) but we didn't."[143] A backing track for this ballad was recorded during the *Double Fantasy* sessions but was not completed. The song was later released on Yoko's *Season of Glass* album.

### "FORGIVE ME, MY LOVE"

This song was reportedly tracked during the *Double Fantasy* sessions, but wasn't released in any form until a version recorded in 1982 turned up on the multi-disc *Onobox* set in 1992.

### "LONELINESS"

Arranger Tony Davilio[144] includes "**Loneliness**" on his of songs recorded for *Double Fantasy*, so we can assume that it was a serious contender for the album. This song was recorded for the unreleased *A Story* album in 1974. Yoko re-recorded it for *It's Alright*.

---

143   Ibid.

144   Davilio

## "IT HAPPENED"

A recording that dated from 1973-74 that was chosen as the B-side to the **"Walking on Thin Ice"** single, perhaps due to the eerie relevance of the lyrics. John, Yoko, and Jack Douglas were considering which of Yoko's older recordings, including **"It Happened,"** would be a suitable B-side on the night John was killed.

## "LET ME COUNT THE WAYS" AND "MILK AND HONEY" SONGS

**"Let Me Count the Ways"** was Yoko's companion piece to John's beautiful Robert Browning-inspired song **"Grow Old with Me."** Yoko's song takes its lyric from Elizabeth Browning's sonnet of the same name. John wrote his song in Bermuda in early June after Yoko played **"Let Me Count the Ways"** for him over the phone. His song takes the first two lines of Robert Browning's poem "Rabbi Ben Ezra" for its lyrical starting point. In her liner notes to *Milk and Honey*, Yoko wrote that she and John envisioned a lavish arrangement for **"Grow Old with Me,"** and they didn't want to do a "rush job" on it just to ensure that it was done in time to be included on *Double Fantasy*, which needed to be released well before Christmas 1980. Thus, **"Let Me Count the Ways"** and **"Grow Old with Me"** were never properly recorded in the studio, and both were released in their demo form on *Milk and Honey* in 1984. Their absence from *Double Fantasy* is especially notable given the fact that the his/hers byplay concept at the heart of *Double Fantasy* originated with these songs.

Yoko discussed her other songs on *Milk and Honey* in a 1984 interview, revealing that with the exception of You're the One, John was familiar with all of them:

" **'Don't Be Scared'** we debated about putting on *Double Fantasy*. **'Sleepless Night'** is a song John liked. **'O Sanity'** was one he always giggled on. **'Your Hands'** he liked very much and that nearly went on *Double Fantasy*. I collected all the songs that had something to do with John…"[145]

Other Yoko songs from *Season of Glass* with which John would have been familiar include **"Toyboat," "She Gets Down on Her Knees," "Will You Touch Me," "Dogtown,"** and **"Turn of the Wheel."** These songs were written in the mid-'70s or earlier, with many intended for Yoko's unreleased album, *A Story*, which was recorded in 1974 while she and John were apart.

---

145   Richard Cook, "Yoko Ono: We Are Only One," *New Musical Express*, February 11, 1984.

## THE REV. JAMES MCCLAIN
### "Somebody Somewhere Need the Lord"

McClain became an ordained Pentecostal minister in 1974. In 1980 he was working security at the Hit Factory when John and Yoko were recording **Double Fantasy**. His story reflects John's ability to connect with people regardless of their station in life.

It was McClain's job to get John and Yoko safely through the crowd that would usually gather outside the Hit Factory—which was located on W. 48th St. a few steps from Eighth Ave.—and up to the studio on the sixth floor. He recalled that sessions often started in the late afternoon and ended at 3 or 4 a.m. when McClain would escort John and Yoko down to their car. Although he never carried a gun, McClain was a big heavyset man that not many people would want to mess with. He later recalled that if he saw someone who looked suspicious—which was often—he would aggressively question them, asking to see ID, and wanting to know why they were there. Even so, he later said there were never any real problems.

McClain said that meeting John inspired him to record an album of his own gospel compositions, something that had been a lifelong ambition.

In 1981, McClain spoke of John:

> "He didn't know how much he helped me. He left a big impact as far as songwriting was concerned. He found out I was a musician and I sang him a few bars of gospel. 'Wow, James!' John said, "You have a nice voice. I want to hear your record.

You got some stuff I can hear?' So I gave him a tape of thirteen songs and he liked them so much he carried the cassette around. He told me to make sure to get him a copy of the single I was working on, "**Somebody Somewhere Need the Lord**," but he died a month before I was finished.[146]

McClain's 45 "Can You Hear Me Lord" was produced by Eddie Germano and recorded at the Hit Factory. John would have another encounter with gospel music in the coming months, and compose a gospel song of his own. Maybe the inspiration he gave McClain worked both ways.

According to McClain, John refused his offer to provide him security around the clock. Speaking of John's murder McClain stated: "If only I had been there, maybe I could have helped."

A photo of McClain with John can be found online.

---

146    Bill Carlton, "Lennon's Memory Shines On: Late Rock Star Inspires Rock of Ages," *New York Daily News,* December 22, 1981.

# FALL

STRANGE TIME, THE FALL OF 1980; certainly, in retrospect, but even at the time it seemed like changes were afoot.

Speculation about "Who Shot J.R.?" was the rage that autumn, a reference to the cliffhanger from the spring on the popular primetime soap opera *Dallas* in which the main character, the ruthless yet eminently fun to watch J.R. Ewing (played by Larry Hagman, who had gained fame in the 1960s as the star of *I Dream of Jeannie*) had been shot. John was a fan of the show and referred to the "Who Shot J.R.?" guessing game in his *Playboy* interview in explaining that, like *Dallas*, one had to follow his and Yoko's music to see what would happen next in the story. Delayed by a writers strike, the first show of the new season didn't air until Friday, November 21, when an estimated 350 million viewers around the world tuned in to find out the answer. (It was Kristen.)

On September 22 Iraq invaded Iran, the start of a protracted eight-year war that would claim an estimated 500,000 total causalities before ending in a stalemate.

Irene Cara's **"Out Here on My Own"** was on the *Billboard* Hot 100 chart all that autumn, getting as high as no. 19 in November, and still on the chart in early December. **"Out Here on My Own"** was co-written by singer Leslie Gore (of **"It's My Party"** fame) and her brother Michael and was featured in the movie *Fame*. The song stands out from other songs on the chart that fall in that its sparsely orchestrated with just a piano to accompany Cara's vocal singing its haunting melody. Perhaps it's only in retrospect, but this song seems to capture some of the foreboding atmosphere of those days. Cara had her first hit with the **title song** of the movie *Fame* in the summer of 1980, which got to no. 4 on the *Billboard* Hot 100. **"Out Here on My Own"** was nominated for an Oscar for Best Original Song, but lost to (what else?) **"Fame."** Cara would go on to greater heights in 1983 when she sang and co-wrote another film song,

"Flashdance … What a Feeling," which was a no. 1 hit in the U.S. and many other countries.

John had heard Diana Ross's "**I'm Coming Out**" in June at a disco in Bermuda[147] the same night he'd heard the B-52s' "**Rock Lobster**." "**I'm Coming Out**" was on Ross's *Diana* album, her collaboration with Chic's Nile Rodgers and Bernard Edwards that is by far her most successful album as a solo artist. The first single from the album, "**Upside Down**," dominated the U.S. *Billboard* Hot 100 during the fall, staying at no. 1 for four weeks from early September to early October. It also topped the R&B chart for four weeks. "**I'm Coming Out**" followed it, peaking at no. 5. Rodgers and Edwards wrote both "**Upside Down**" and "**I'm Coming Out**" in addition to producing *Diana*. Disco may have been dead, but dance music was still alive. "**I'm Coming Out**" became an LBGTQ[148] anthem and Ross has opened her shows with the song in the ensuing decades. "**I'm Coming Out**" was at no. 9 on the December 6 *Billboard* Hot 100 chart, three positions behind John's "**(Just Like) Starting Over**."

The second biggest song in the U.S. that fall was Barbra Streisand's "**Woman in Love**." It stayed at no. 1 for three weeks starting on October 25 (the day after John's "**(Just Like) Starting Over**" single was released) through the first half of November. It was still in the top five in early December. For a song that expresses a woman's determination to love the object of her desire, this a very moody and melancholy song. As was the case with most of the songs on the *Guilty* album, "**Woman in Love**" was written by Barry and Robin Gibb, proof that the Bee Gees had not really left the scene. Like Chic's Rodgers and Edwards, the disco backlash hadn't prevented them from writing and producing hits for other artists.

---

147   Seaman

148   This acronym was not yet in wide use in 1980.

Barry also produced *Guilty*, and his duet with Barbra on the **title track** was at no. 14 on the Billboard chart of December 6. **"Woman in Love"** is Streisand's last U.S. no. 1 single to date.

Streisand had a long history with John and the Beatles. She organized an April 1973 L.A. fundraiser to help pay the legal fees of Daniel Ellsberg, who had leaked the Vietnam era "Pentagon Papers" to the *New York Times* in 1971. The event drew not only John and Yoko, but also George and Ringo, making it one of the few times three Beatles were in the same place at the same time during the 1970s. Streisand has recorded many Lennon and Beatles songs through the years, including tackling **Mother** in 1971. Both John and Yoko loved Streisand's song **"The Way We Were,"** which topped the U.S. charts for three weeks in early 1974, and the movie of the same name in which she co-starred with Robert Redford.

The Korgis' **"Everybody's Got to Learn Sometime"** is a moody, somewhat mysterious number. This song was at no. 21 on *Billboard's* December 6 Hot 100 chart. In September it had gotten no. 5 in the U.K., increasing the likelihood that John was aware of it. The song had an unusually long shelf life, topping the singles chart in France in August of 1980 and then repeating the feat in Spain during the spring of 1981. The band have cited John's early '70s music as an influence on **"Everybody's Got to Learn Sometime"** and other songs they've recorded.

The Police had a huge hit in the U.K. that fall when **"Don't Stand so Close to Me"** hit no.1 on September 27 and stayed atop the chart for four weeks. The first single from the band's third album *Zenyatta Mondatta*, "Don't Stand So Close to Me" has a very dark mood as it tells a story of potential affair between a teacher and a student. That such subject matter was in a hit song that year reminds us how much certain attitudes have changed in forty years. Demonstrating the necessity of a good thesaurus on a songwriter's bookshelf, songwriter Sting rhymes Nabokov (the novelist of *Lolita* fame) with "shake and cough."

In the U.K. The Jam, a band that wore its Mod 1960s inspiration proudly, had their second no. 1 hit in September with "**Start**," a great song that specifically referenced the Beatles' "Revolver" track, George Harrison's "**Taxman**."

Robert Palmer's "**Johnny and Mary**"—a strange, somewhat ominous, song—was on the radio that autumn. The song features a modern sounding rhythm track, but is uncharacteristically downbeat for a song with a danceable beat. The lyric relates that "Johnny" is "always running around trying to find certainty' and "he needs all the world to confirm that he ain't lonely." Palmer had a U.S. top twenty hit in the summer of 1979 with "**Bad Case of Loving You (Doctor Doctor)**." Although it failed to crack the top 40 in the U.S., "**Johnny and Mary**" went on to top the Spanish singles chart for five weeks in the spring of 1981.

Stevie Wonder's "**Master Blaster (Jammin')**" was Stevie's Bob Marley tribute, released while the Marley was still with us. The song grew out of a joint appearance that Stevie and Marley made at the inaugural Black Music Association conference in Philadelphia in June of 1979, when Stevie joined Marley on stage. It was at number 5 on *Billboard's* Hot 100 chart of December 6, 1980, one spot ahead of John's "**(Just Like) Starting Over**" at no. 6. Marley was scheduled to open shows for Stevie on his *Hotter than July* tour that fall but Marley's illness meant he couldn't tour. Stevie paid touching tribute to John when he informed his concert audience of John's death.

An examination of *Billboard's* top 10 songs on the last day of his life validates John's belief back at the beginning of the year that the music scene of 1980 would be hospitable for veteran artists like himself. Eight of the ten artists had their first hits in the 1960s. These included Kenny

Rogers, Barbra Streisand, Stevie, John, Neil Diamond (whose "**Love on the Rocks**" was at no. 7 just behind John at no. 6), Diana Ross and Cliff Richard. The two other songs were Leo Sayer's cover of the Crickets 1960 song "**More Than I Can Say**," and Bruce Springsteen's "**Hungry Heart**," a retro piece that featured vocals by Mark Volman and Howard Kaylan of 1960s hitmakers, the Turtles.

On Tuesday November 4, former actor and ex-California governor Ronald Reagan ousted U.S. President Jimmy Carter in a landslide vote, with Carter winning just six states plus the District of Columbia. The hostage crisis in Iran had dominated U.S. politics for the preceding year, and Reagan capitalized on Carter's inability to free them, as well as voter's discontent with inflation and a recession that had gripped the country for close to a year. Reagan had built his political career opposing the liberal agenda of the 1960s counterculture, and many saw his election as a repudiation of the activism of the 1960s. It would be hard to deny that the country had taken a rightward turn, as Republicans won control of the U.S. Senate for the first time since 1954. Even though many of the social changes initiated in the '60s, including civil rights, women's rights, environmental activism, and gay rights were embedded in the culture by 1980, the "Reagan Revolution" had arrived. Most historians agree that, similar to the 1932 election that swept Franklin Roosevelt the Democrats into power, the 1980 election represented a realignment in American politics, the fallout from which would resonate for decades.

There are photos of John, Yoko, and Sean apparently watching President Carter's motorcade pass by the Dakota that October. Although John and Yoko had attended Carter's inaugural gala in Washington D.C. in January 1977, Fred Seaman reported[149] that John had grown disenchanted with what he saw as Carter's pious moralizing and said he would

---

149   https://www.dailymail.co.uk/news/article-2009562/John-Lennon-closet-conservative-fan-Reagan.html

vote for Reagan had he been eligible to do so as a U.S. citizen. Seaman went on to state his opinion that the 1980 Lennon was a changed man and now somewhat embarrassed by his radical years of the early '70s. The lack of anything approaching a political statement in his last batch of studio recordings does nothing to undercut that statement.

John told *Newsweek* that fall:

> "What the hell was I doing (in the early 1970s) fighting the American government just because (American radical) Jerry Rubin couldn't get what he wanted—a cushy job."[150]

In a highly publicized sign of the times, Rubin had recently taken a "straight" job in the business world.

John's anti-voting stance and skepticism that cigarette smoking causes lung cancer (both he and Yoko smoked like chimneys) were two head-scratching statements he made in his 1980 interviews.

It must be pointed out that in the final week of his life John joined Yoko in issuing a statement of support of the mostly Japanese-American workers on strike in San Francisco and Los Angeles against the Japan Foods Corporation, a subsidiary of the Japanese multinational Kikkoman. Yoko's cousin was among the workers demanding pay commensurate with what white workers earned, and it was through his entreaty that John and Yoko got involved. They even had plans to fly to San Francisco to attend a rally in support of the workers, and to also visit with farm-workers union leader Cesar Chavez and make what Yoko later described as "a human rights statement for migrant farm workers." These hardly seem like the actions of a newly minted conservative.

Yoko recalled that "their bags were packed" and speaking of the San

---

150   Graustark

JOHN LENNON : 1980 PLAYLIST

Francisco rally John told her "I'm going to stand there with my Asian wife holding my Eurasian son in my arms."[151]. This would have been John's first public activism in many years.

John had met Reagan in the fall of 1974 at an NFL football game in Los Angeles, and the unlikely pair seemed to hit it off. *Monday Night Football* announcer Frank Gifford would later recall the future president sitting with his arm on John's shoulder explaining the fine points of the American game. In his December 1980 interview with *Rolling Stone's* Jonathan Cott, John noted something he had in common with Reagan: that he referred to Yoko as "'Mother,' like our president-elect (Reagan) calls his wife 'Mommy.'" Just months after John's murder Reagan was nearly killed in a March 30, 1981 assassination attempt. Fate would have many Americans learning of John's assassination via a *Monday Night Football* broadcast when Howard Cosell delivered the tragic news. Cosell had conducted an insightful radio interview with John in September of 1974, and had invited John to visit him in "Our *Monday Night (Football)* booth" at the close of the interview. John had (accurately) described Cosell as a "ham" in a 1976 correspondence with a fan.

On December 4, Led Zeppelin announced that they were breaking up due to the death of drummer John Bonham on September 25. "Bonzo"—who by one account[152] had once done heroin with John at New York's Plaza Hotel in the mid-'70s—died following a bout of heavy drinking during rehearsals for Zeppelin's North American tour. So, the biggest band of the '70s and the biggest band of the '60s both lost members that fall, ending Zeppelin in its prime and foreclosing the possibility of future reunions for the Beatles.

On Saturday night December 6, while John was having dinner at Mr.

---

151   Yoko Ono ImaginePeace.com (Spring 2004)

152   Goldman

Chow's with the crew who'd done the BBC interview, a young band from Dublin was making their U.S. debut at The Ritz club downtown. It's doubtful that many of the twenty-five or so people in attendance could imagine that U2 would one day soon be the biggest band in the world. At the height of their popularity during their 1987 *Joshua Tree* tour, the band took the stage to John's "**Stand by Me,**" an emotional moment that made their admiration for him unmistakable. And it wasn't just about music. Like John, U2's Bono would attempt—and succeed—to use the band's worldwide popularity to bring about some good in the world.

---

## THE BENNY CUMMINGS SINGERS & THE KINGS TEMPLE CHOIR

"It Is Well with My Soul"

On September 11th, these two gospel choirs were gathered at A & R Studios on Seventh Avenue to overdub vocals onto Yoko's song "**Hard Times Are Over.**" A & R was used because it could better accommodate the 20-30 people that made up the combined choirs. John was especially moved as the group joined hands in prayer before they began singing. With their task completed, the leader stepped forward and said into the microphone: "Mr. Lennon, we have something we would like to give you." The group then sang "**It Is Well with My Soul,**" a traditional hymn from their repertoire. Assistant engineer Julie Last later described the performance as "slow and achingly beautiful."[153]

Composed in 1893 by Phillip Bliss with words by Horatio Spafford, the song grew out of Spafford's tragically losing all four of his daughters when their ship sank while crossing the Atlantic. This occurred after Spafford had lost his son in the Chicago Fire of 1873, an event that ruined him financially.

"**It Is Well with My Soul**" offers believers reassurance that no matter what trials befall them, they have been redeemed by Christ's death and "The sky, not the grave, is our goal." The moving performance left both John and Yoko with tears in their eyes. Jack Douglas later called it

---

153   Sharp *Starting Over*

"an incredible session … it was so spiritual."[154]

It's interesting to speculate if this experience might have played a role in two songs John composed in his last weeks of his life, "**Help Me to Help Myself**" and "**You Saved My Soul**." "**You Saved My Soul**" dates from mid-November and was the last new song John committed to tape, and likely the last composition of his astonishing songwriting career. Accompanying himself on electric guitar, John thanks Yoko for saving him from "my suicide." However, instead of thanking her for saving his life, he thanks her for saving his "soul," perhaps indicating that the suicide was contemplated due to a spiritual crisis.

If anything, "**Help Me to Help Myself**" is an even more harrowing song, so much so that one wonders if it would have seen the light of day if John were still alive. The song was among the original recordings made public on the *Lost Lennon Tapes* radio series that started in 1988, and it was included as a bonus track on the 2000 twentieth anniversary reissue of **Double Fantasy**. In lyrics that are chillingly prescient, John sings:

*I tried so hard to stay alive*

*But the angel of destruction keeps on hounding me, all around*

Against gospel-like piano chords, John implores "Oh help me Lord…" It's difficult to think of another song in the Lennon oeuvre with the hymn-like quality of "**Help Me to Help Myself**." This marks the second time in 1980—"**Living on Borrowed Time**" being the first instance—that John explicitly predicts that he is not long for this world. In addition, his last artistic contribution would be his guitar and production work on Yoko's foreboding "**Walking on Thin Ice**" in the days before his death.

---

154   Ibid

Sometime after returning from Bermuda, John composed and demoed the song "**Gone From this Place**." (He sings a bit of the song during a late August overdub sessions for "**(Just Like) Starting Over.**") Its chorus contains the repeated lines "Ah, I don't want to die."

Strange days indeed. Cue the theremin.

When "**Help Me to Help Myself**" was released in 2000, Yoko had this to say about the song in an interview with the U.K. *Independent*:

> "He was playing this on the piano at home, half-laughing and saying 'Wouldn't it be something if we ever put this out?' They say that people start to think of God near death. It's possible that was the case here. Whatever he was thinking he was doing; it is a beautiful song and I wanted to share it…"[155]

---

155   Chris Gray, "Death Themes in Lennon's Last Songs," *Independent*, October 10,2000, https://www.independent.co.uk/arts-entertainment/music/news/death-themes-in-lennons-last-songs-638298.html

ELTON JOHN

"Little Jeannie"

"Sartorial Eloquence (Don't You Wanna Play This Game No More?)"

"Sorry Seems to be the Hardest Word"

Elton played before an estimated crowd of 450,000 in New York's Central Park on Saturday, September 13. Prior to playing John's "**Imagine**," Elton told the crowd:

> "We're going to do a song written by a friend of mine who I haven't seen for a long time, but it's a very beautiful song. You all know it. He only lives just over the road and he hasn't made a record for ages, (but) he's doing one at the moment."

Given that fact that this show was held on the park's Great Lawn, which is across Central Park West and up about ten blocks from the Dakota, it was almost literally in John's backyard. In his 2019 memoir *Me*[156] Elton wrote that John and Yoko unexpectedly showed up at the after-show party, which was held on a ship called the *Peking*, a "floating museum" on the East River. Elton noted that John was "hilarious as ever" and "full of excitement about making a new album." Unfortunately, Elton was exhausted after the show and left the party early. It was the last time he would ever see John.

In a 1975 *Rolling Stone* interview, John recalled the first time he

---

156    Elton John, *Me* (New York: Henry Holt, 2019)

heard Elton's music:

> "I remember hearing … '**Your Song**' …– it was one of Elton's first big hits—and remember thinking "Great, that's the first new thing that's happened since we happened." It was a step forward. There was something about his vocals that was an improvement on all the English vocals until then. I was pleased with it."[157]

John became good friends with Elton in 1974 during his separation from Yoko. Elton sang and played on John's "**Whatever Gets You Thru the Night**" while John returned the favor for Elton's cover of "**Lucy in the Sky with Diamonds**" (on which John suggested that Elton do the middle part of the song with a reggae beat), both of which were no. 1 *Billboard* singles in the U.S. John joined Elton and his band onstage at Madison Square Garden on Thanksgiving night, 1974. They performed "**Lucy in the Sky with Diamonds**" and "**Whatever Gets You Thru the Night**" and John sang lead on the Beatles "**I Saw Her Standing There**." John and Bernie Taupin later returned to the stage to play tambourines during the encore of Elton's current hit "**The Bitch Is Back**."[158] Elton would later recall that John was creative and full of fun during 1974, a description at odds with the "Lost Weekend" narrative that John and Yoko would later construct.

On the Wednesday after the Central Park concert Elton appeared

---

157   *The Ballad of John and Yoko* 1975 interview with Pete Hamill "Long Night's Journey Into Day" June 5, 1975.

158   The appearance with Elton is often incorrectly described as John's final public performance. That designation goes to the "Salute to Sir Lew Grade"   at which John performed on April 18, 1975. Before an audience at New York's Waldorf Astoria and accompanied by a backing band, John performed "**Imagine**," "**Stand By Me**," and "**Slippin' and Slidin'**." John had a checkered history with Grade's ATV publishing company, which was reflected by the two-faced headgear worn by his backing band.

on the *Tomorrow Show* with Tom Snyder. Elliot Mintz once said that two shows that John never missed were *The Tonight Show* with Johnny Carson and the *Tomorrow Show* with Tom Snyder. (Snyder's show followed Johnny's on NBC, broadcast on Channel 4 in New York.) Elton performs affecting solo piano versions of "his hit from this summer" as Snyder describes it, "**Little Jeanie**," and his current single "**Sartorial Eloquence (Don't You Wanna Play This Game No More?)**." Both songs were from Elton's *21 at 33* album, which had been released in May.

During his interview with Snyder, Elton breaks into the song "**Cartier**," an amusing ditty that was the B-side to "**Sartorial Eloquence**" in the U.S.

"**Little Jeannie**" was a something of a comeback song for Elton. It was his biggest U.S. hit in four years since he and Kiki Dee hit no. 1 with "**Don't Go Breaking My Heart**" in 1976, and his biggest solo hit since 1975's "**Island Girl**." In the interim he had declared his bisexuality in a 1977 *Rolling Stone* article, something that almost certainly damaged his career in the U.S.

On November 6, Elton appeared on the *Tonight Show* in L.A. Before being interviewed by host Johnny Carson, Elton performed a solo piano rendition of his 1976 hit "**Sorry Seems to Be the Hardest Word**." This was something of a curious choice given that Elton still had *21 at 33* to promote.

Elton and Bernie Taupin later wrote the song "Empty Garden" about John. Yoko and Sean joined Elton onstage during a performance of the song at Madison Square Garden in 1982.

---

## DONNA SUMMER
"The Wanderer"

While visiting John and Yoko at the Dakota in September 1980, *Los Angeles Times* music critic Robert Hilburn[159] reported that John excitedly entered Yoko's office brandishing a copy of Donna Summer's new single "**The Wanderer**" (not to be confused with the old Dion song) and shouted "Listen!" Putting the 45 on the record player he said "She's doing Elvis!" Indeed, Summer appropriates the King's vocal mannerisms in the song, just as John had done on his own "**Starting Over**." John may have taken this as confirmation that his instincts were right in suspecting that the music of the musical heroes of his youth was back in vogue.

Summer was newly signed to David Geffen's eponymous new record label, and she and John were about to become label-mates. "**The Wanderer**" was written by Summer and renowned disco producer Giorgio Moroder. Despite this pedigree, the song marked a turn toward synth-heavy new wave and away from disco for the lady known as "The Queen of Disco." Summer was no doubt responding to the changing marketplace since by this time disco had been on the wane in the U.S. for over a year, after having dominated the charts for several years.

David Geffen later recalled[160] that Summer's song "**Cold Love**," a track from *The Wanderer* that had just been released as a single, was among the topics he and John discussed at the Record Plant early in the

---

159    Robert Hilburn, *Cornflakes with John Lennon*, (New York: Rodale books, 2010)

160    Kurt Loder, "The Last Session," *Rolling Stone,* January 22, 1981

evening of December 8th. Although it featured a rock sound reminiscent of her smash hit "**Hot Stuff**," "**Cold Love**" would fail to match the success of that song or "**The Wanderer**," stalling at no. 33 on the Billboard "Hot 100."

Even though "**The Wanderer**" reached #3 on the *Billboard* singles chart, time would show that it marked the beginning of the end of Summer's remarkable run of chart success. After 1980, she only hit the U.S. top 10 three more times throughout the rest of her career. She was 63 when she died of lung cancer in 2012.

JOHN LENNON : 1980 PLAYLIST

---

NEIL YOUNG

"My My, Hey Hey (*Out of the Blue*)"

"Hey Hey My My (*Into the Black*)"


"My My" is the acoustic version, "Hey Hey" is the electric one. Both songs bookended Young's highly successful 1979 album ***Rust Never Sleeps***, a phrase which is taken from the lyrics of these songs. In both Young opines "It's better to burn out than to fade away." John took issue with this sentiment when responding to a question about punk rock in his *Playboy* interview. Saying that while he loved "all this punky stuff. It's pure. I'm not ... crazy about the people who destroy themselves." [161]

Both of Young's songs name-check Sex Pistols singer Johnny Rotten as an example of someone who burned out before he could "fade away." The Pistols had imploded on the heels of their first U.S. tour in early 1978. By the time of John's interview Rotten had reverted to his real name John Lydon and was making music with his new band Public Image Ltd. In other words, it was inaccurate to say he'd "burned out" after the Pistols imploded.

Asked by interviewer David Sheff about Young's "Better to burn out..." line, John stated:

> "I hate it. It's better to fade away like an old soldier than to burn out. I don't appreciate worship of dead Sid Vicious or dead Jim Morrison or dead John Wayne. Making Sid Vicious a hero

---

161   Sheff

or Jim Morrison … it's garbage to me. I worship the people who survive. (Actresses) Gloria Swanson (then 81), Greta Garbo (then 75). Sid Vicious died for what? So that we might rock? I mean, it's garbage. … If Neil Young admires that sentiment so much, why doesn't he do it? Because he sure as hell faded away and came back many times, like all of us. No thank you. I'll take the living and the healthy."[162]

The erstwhile bassist of the Sex Pistols, Vicious died from a heroin overdose in February 2, 1979, while out on bail on charges that he'd stabbed his girlfriend Nancy Spungen to death in October 1978. Both incidents received extensive publicity in New York tabloids and John had obviously followed Vicious' travails closely. As fate would have it, Sid died on in an apartment on Bank St. in Greenwich Village, the same street on which John and Yoko lived when they first came to the U.S

It's also possible that John was also thinking of the suicide death of Ian Curtis, the singer of the emerging post-punk British band Joy Division the previous May. Curtis hanged himself the day before the band were going to leave for their first U.S. tour. An avid follower of the British music scene, John may have been aware of Curtis' fate, even though Joy Division were not well known in the U.S. at the time.

John's oft stated admiration for punk rock and new wave artists must have been tempered by the fact that contemporaries of his, including Elton John and Rod Stewart, were the among targets of the Sex Pistols wrath. On the other hand, John was something of a godfather to the punk movement, which harkened back to concise, tuneful songs that were often served with a generous portion of rage. It's worth noting that punk and new wave sprang up at a time when John was no longer making

---

162   Sheff

music and had left a void in his absence. Champions of punk rock including Ira Robbins of *The Trouser Press* and Dave Marsh of *Rolling Stone* both penned open letters to John during his absence imploring him to return to making music. In a sense, John was a spiritual godfather to the entire punk/new wave movement.

Although several of Yoko's ***Double Fantasy*** tracks such as "**Kiss, Kiss, Kiss**" (and subsequently "**Walking on Thin Ice**") bore a New Wave influence, John's new songs—with the notable exception of "**I'm Losing You**"—were bereft of his old bitterness and anger. John explained that he was a different person in 1980 than he was when he recorded the "primal scream" ***Plastic Ono Band*** album ten years earlier, and this maturity and contentment was reflected in his music.

In an eerie bit of synchronicity, Darby Crash, the singer of the L.A. punk band the Germs, OD'd and died on December 7, 1980.

As for Young, John had been an admirer of his since the start of his career. John was said to own a copy of the first ***Buffalo Springfield*** album, which was released in 1966. That record features classic Young compositions including "**Flying on the Ground Is Wrong**," "**Burned**," and "**Nowadays Clancy Can't Even Sing**."

Speaking to *Rolling Stone* in 1970, John said of Young: "...You can pick him out a mile away, the whole style. He writes some nice songs.[163]

Young played the Beatles "**A Day in the Life**" on the PA prior to his shows on his 1978 ***Rust Never Sleeps*** tour. In later years he's often performed the song in concert, most memorably when Paul McCartney guested with him to sing his lines from the song at London's Hyde Park in June 2009. Young has referenced John in two of his late career songs, "Peace and Love" from *Mirror Ball*, and "Devil's Sidewalk" from *Greendale*.

---

163   Wenner

# THE PUNK ROCK MOVIE

## THE SEX PISTOLS
"God Save the Queen"

## THE CLASH
"White Riot"

Other than decrying the hero worship of the recently departed Sid Vicious to *Playboy*, John had surprisingly little to say about the two biggest punk bands – the Sex Pistols and the Clash – during his 1980 interviews. When he did mention them, he said that he had seen videos of both bands performing. This was an unusual thing to say at the time, since MTV had yet to be founded and in 1980 most people still experienced music mainly by listening to records or playing the radio.

Photographer Bob Gruen was friendly with John and later revealed that he'd lent John a tape of new wave bands shot by director Don Letts, who was a friend of his. This tape was very likely Letts' film *The* Punk Rock Movie, which had been released in 1978. In early December John left word for Gruen that he'd enjoyed the tape.

Letts shot most of the film on Super 8 film at the Roxy club in London where he was the deejay. All of the footage dates from 1977, so it captures the U.K. punk scene at its height. The Sex Pistols footage is from their April 3, 1977 show The Screen on the Green Theater in London. It happened to be Sid Vicious' first show with the band after replacing bassist Glen Matlock. Reports had it that Matlock had been sacked because he was a Beatles fan, although Matlock later said he wanted to leave the band..

*The Punk Rock Movie* kicks off with the Sex Pistols performing their "tribute" to Queen Elizabeth, **God Save the Queen**, a song that sold hundreds of thousands of copies despite being banned by the BBC. It's a powerful performance. The song is reprised to close out the movie where it is preceded by four Pistols songs: **I'm a Lazy Sod**, **Pretty Vacant**, **Liar**, and **New York**. John had his own run in with Queen Elizabeth in 1969 when he returned his M.B.E. award in protest of the British government's involvement in the "Nigeria-Biafra thing" (a war) and the U.S. war in Vietnam.

By 1980 the Sex Pistols had been disbanded for two years following their tumultuous U.S. tour in early 1978. Asked in his BBC interview if he's heard the Sex Pistols music, John replied:

> "Only whatever they did a video of it (sic). There were a lot of videos of them hanging out at Max's[164] or wherever the hell they were hanging out and playing. Johnny Rotten and all that. (I thought) yeah, great! To me, initially on impact seeing all that I thought That's how we used to behave at the Cavern before Brian told us to stop throwing up and sleeping on stage and swearing'...But still, yeah I think it's *great*! I absolutely do."[165]

John clearly identified with the Pistols desire to lift a middle finger toward society's revered institutions such as the British monarchy. The Pistols' decision to play small venues in the southern U.S. to start

---

164   Recall that Max's Kansas City was the punk club where John saw Devo in 1977.

165   Lennon, Ono, Peebles

their brief tour in January 1978 seemed an art "happening" of a sort that welcomed confrontation with their audience. Although John had the mistaken impression that the Pistols had played at the famous downtown club Max's Kansas City, (in fact, they'd yet to play a show in New York), he was no doubt thinking about the shows that Sid Vicious performed at the club in the September of 1978 with a pick-up band that included ex-New York Dolls Jerry Nolan and Arthur Kane.

The Clash are represented with three songs in *The Punk Rock Movie*, live versions of **White Riot** and **Garageland**, both of which are on their first album, *The Clash*, released the U.K. in 1977. They also perform **1977**, which was released as **White Riot's** b-side. John told Robert Hilburn in October: "Someone showed me a video of the Clash. They're good."[166] John said this in the context of explaining that he loved the current music scene, saying "It's the best period since the 1960s."

Following the success of their *London Calling* album earlier in the year, The Clash released their fourth studio album, the three record *Sandinista!* on December 12, 1980, just four days following John's murder. The album was named for the left-wing government of Nicaragua, which had overthrown longtime dictator Anastasio Somoza DeBayle in July 1979.

Other notable artists included in *The Punk Rock Movie* include legendary New York punks Johnny Thunders (formerly of the New York Dolls) and the Heartbreakers performing **Born to Lose** and **Chinese Rocks**; Siouxsie and the Banshees with **Bad Shape**; and a young Billy Idol leading Generation X singing **Walking in the City**. In 1983 Siouxsie would have a no. 3 U.K. hit with their cover of John's *White Album* song Dear Prudence.

---

166   Hilburn

# THANKSGIVING 1980

There are photos of John and his family celebrating a traditional Thanksgiving dinner at their house in Cold Spring Harbor, NY, in 1979, so his years on American soil had gotten him into the habit of celebrating the holiday. New York's Macy's Thanksgiving Day Parade passed by the Dakota each year (and still does) so it's likely John would watch the annual television broadcast, which features performers outside of the Macy's flagship store on 33rd St.

The musical performers on the show in 1980 included Stephanie Mills singing her hit song "**Never Knew Love Like This Before,**" which was at no. 6 on the *Billboard* Hot 100 on this day. The song would win the Best R&B Song award at the 1981 Grammys for songwriters Reggie Lewis and James Mtume. Lewis would leave a huge imprint on the music of the 1980s a couple of years later when he produced most of the tracks on Madonna's debut album, and wrote her hit song "Borderline," a song not dissimilar in feel to "**Never Knew Love Like This Before**."

Also performing (okay, lip-syncing) were Sister Sledge doing their huge 1979 hit "**We Are Family.**" How huge? Well, per *Billboard* it was the second biggest song of 1979 in the U.S., behind Donna Summer's "**Hot Stuff.**" "**We Are Family**" was written by Bernard Edwards and Nile Rodgers of Chic, and would become a ubiquitous presence at weddings in the coming decades.

The Spinners were one of the most successful R&B groups of the 1970s. At the parade they performed their cover of Sam Cooke's 1961 hit **"Cupid"** (now combined with **"I've Loved You for a Long Time"**), which had risen to no. 4 on the *Billboard* singles chart during the summer. John had taped himself singing Cooke's 1957 hit **"You Send Me"** at the Dakota in 1979. **"Cupid/I've Loved You for a Long Time"** would prove to be the end of the Spinners' long string of hits.

Child actress Danielle Brisebois sang the then-ubiquitous song **"Tomorrow"** from the long-running Broadway show *Annie*.

The telecast also featured Linda Ronstadt and Rex Smith singing a couple of numbers from Gilbert and Sullivan's ***The Pirates of Penzance***, a Public Theater production that had debuted to great acclaim in Central Park the previous July, and would soon move to Broadway in January 1981.

Ronstadt had a good 1980 with two top 10 U.S. hits, **"How Do I Make You"** and her cover of Little Anthony and the Imperials' **"Hurt So Bad"** from her album ***Mad Love***, a seeming response to New Wave that featured three Elvis Costello covers. She also sang on the Dirt Band's cover of Rodney Crowell's **An American Dream**, which got to no. 13 in the spring. Ronstadt wouldn't have another top 10 hit in the U.S. until her duet with Aaron Neville, "Don't Know Much," got to no. 2 in 1989.

For a man whose activities have been so exhaustively documented, there is scant information on how John spent his last Thanksgiving just ten days before his death. After having spent the previous day filming video in both Central Park and at a gallery in Soho for a prospective video for **"Starting Over,"** it is likely John and Yoko chose to spend a quiet day at home. Some have speculated that they met with Ringo—who was staying at the Plaza—during this weekend, but Ringo himself has dated his last meeting with John and Yoko (at the Plaza) to November 15. At that time they made plans for John to contribute songs to and play on Ringo's new album, with recording sessions planned for L.A. in January

1981. These plans were firm enough that Tom Petty later said he was looking forward to meeting John in L.A. because he was recording his album *Hard Promises* at Cherokee Studios, the same facility Ringo was going to use. This was the same studio that John and Ringo had used in April 1976 to record John's song "**Cookin'**" for the ***Ringo's Rotogravure*** album. The U.S. pressings of Petty's *Hard Promises* contains an etched message on the run-out groove that says: "We Love You JL."

BRUCE SPRINGSTEEN

*The River* and "Hungry Heart"

Springsteen was the most important American rock artist to emerge in the 1970s. Bruce was a hometown hero in New York so John was doubtlessly aware of his Phil Spector influenced 1975 breakthrough ***Born to Run*** and its 1978 follow-up ***Darkness on the Edge of Town***. In 1978 old Beatles hand Tony Bramwell was doing promotion for Springsteen and sought to set up a meeting with Bruce and John. Bramwell recalled that the meeting didn't happen because John got "freaked out" and "didn't want to deal with all that fame again."[167]

Fred Seaman later said[168] that John admired Bruce and had asked him for a copy of Bruce's fifth album, ***The River***, which was released in the U.S. on October 17, 1980. Upon listening to the two-record set a downcast John told Seaman "well his is better." "This is fucking great…. This is better than ***Double Fantasy***."

***The River*** was a product of nearly two years of recording sessions. Bruce scrapped an earlier one-disc version of the album in the fall of 1979 and returned to the studio for more recording. The 1979 album was officially released in 2015 as part of *The Ties That Bind* archival project. The twenty tracks on ***The River*** comprise only a fraction of the material recorded during the sessions for the album. An additional twenty-seven

---

167    Phillip Recchia and Lindsay Powers, "Looking Back on John Lennon's NYC Love Affair 35 Years After His Death," December 8, 2005, https://nypost.com/2005/12/08/city-apple-of-lennons-eye-death-25-years-ago-ended-love-affair-with-n-y/

168    Seaman quoted on Fabcast Podcast "Summer 1980: Coming up on Borrowed Time."

songs from the sessions have seen the light of day in the years since, notably on the 1998 *Tracks* box and later on *"The Ties That Bind"* set. Bruce aficionados will tell you that many of these tracks are better than the ones that made the album, and they might be right! This was an incredibly prolific time for Springsteen as a songwriter, when he was at the peak of his creativity. By one estimate there are still twenty songs from these sessions that remain in the vault forty years later.

Springsteen reflected on *The River* in 2009:

> "It was a record made during a recession, hard times in the States. It was a record where I first started to tackle men and women and families and marriage. I took back (the original single album version of *The River*) because I didn't feel it was big enough. I wanted to capture the themes I'd been writing about on *Darkness (on the Edge of Town)* ... and at the same time (add) the music that made our live shows so much fun and enjoyable for our audience."[169]

*The River* had a number of songs apparently inspired by British invasion bands, particularly the Searchers. (Bruce had covered the Searchers hit **"Every Time You Walk into the Room"** in concert.) This was the case with the album's first song, **"The Ties That Bind."** While the album tipped its hat to 1960s musical styles including frat rock (**"Sherry Darling"**), and Tex-Mex (**"Ramrod," "Cadillac Ranch"**), it also touched on darker themes regarding "The distance between ... American promise and American reality" as Springsteen once put it. **"Point Blank," "Wreck on the Highway,"** and even **"Cadillac Ranch"** all explicitly deal with the theme of mortality.

---

169   November 8, 2009 prior to playing *The River* in its entirety at Madison Square Garden.

The *Rolling Stone* review of *The River* was written by Paul Nelson and noted: "What makes *The River* really special is Bruce Springsteen's epic exploration of the second acts of American lives.[170]

In his interview with Jonathan Cott on the night of December 5-6, John said of Bruce: "I haven't seen him … but I've heard such good things about him from people that I respect. And I might actually get out of bed to go watch him." He had just missed a chance a week earlier when Bruce and the E Street Band played two shows at Madison Square Garden during the Thanksgiving weekend. Bruce's U.S. tour to support *The River* had started in the Midwest in early October and would extend into March 1981 before moving on to Europe.

In his final interview on December 8, John pronounced **"Hungry Heart"** to be "a great record," adding "To me it's the same kind of period sound as '**Starting Over**.'"[171] The first single released from *The River,* "Hungry Heart" was climbing the charts at the time. Bruce had written **"Hungry Heart** "for the Ramones after singer Joey Ramone asked if he could write a song for them after Bruce caught their show in Asbury Park in early 1979. Heeding to the entreaties of his manager, Jon Landau, Bruce later decided the song was too good to give away.

**"Hungry Heart"** features stellar background vocals from Mark Volman and Howard Kaylan, former members of the Turtles, a band that had gained success with a Beatles-inspired sound in the mid and late '60s. **"Hungry Heart"** was at no. 8 on the *Billboard* single chart—two places behind John's **"Starting Over"**—during the second week of December.

Springsteen began playing his version of **"Twist and Shout"** during his 1978 tour, always as one of his encores. His version of **"Twist and Shout"** was clearly based on the Beatles' cover version, on which

---

170    Paul Nelson, "The River," *Rolling Stone,* December 11, 1980.

171    Lennon, Ono, Peebles

John sings a raw-throated vocal, rather than the Isley Brothers original. Springsteen continued to play **"Twist and Shout"** regularly in subsequent years and over time it has taken on a Tex-Mex flavor. Among the other Beatles songs he's played live are **"Tell Me Why,"** **"Birthday,"** **"I Saw Her Standing There"** (played with Paul McCartney in 2012) and **"Come Together,"** which he memorably sang with Axl Rose in celebration of John's 1994 induction into the Rock and Roll Hall of Fame as a solo artist.

Bruce was playing a show at the Spectrum in Philadelphia the night of December 8. Taking the Spectrum stage the next night, Bruce stated:

> "It's a hard night to come out and play … when so much has been lost. The first record I ever learned was a record called **'Twist and Shout.'** If it wasn't for John Lennon we'd all be someplace very different tonight. It's a hard world where you get asked to live with a lot of things that are just unlivable. And it's hard to come out and play tonight, but there's nothing else to do."

With that, Bruce and the E Street Band tore into **"Born to Run."**

## THE CARS

"Touch and Go"

On the last afternoon of his life, John praised this inventive and melodic single from the Cars third album, **Panorama.** While being interviewed by RKO Radio, he described the song as being "right out of the '50s. Oh Oh Oh (imitating Cars singer Ric Ocasek's **Touch and Go** vocal) that's New Wave ... a lot of it is '50s stuff, but with '80s styling." John claimed that like **"Touch and Go,"** like his song **"Starting Over,"** was a "'50s song but with an '80s approach."

The Cars may have been on John's mind because they had just played two concerts at Madison Square Garden the previous Wednesday and Thursday. They were also the subject of an October 30 *Rolling Stone* cover story that John likely perused.

**"Touch and Go"** is indeed an excellent song that deserved to be a bigger hit than it was. The song has an usual rhythm in its verses with the bass and drums playing in the 5/4 time signature while the rest of the band plays in 4/4 time, giving the music a weird start/stop effect. Guitarist Elliot Easton contributes a blistering, yet beautifully melodic, guitar solo. Easton recently described **Touch and Go**, and his contributions to it, as one of his proudest moments as a member of the Cars.[172]

On September 19th the Cars performed **"Touch and Go"** and other songs from **Panorama** on the ABC television show *Fridays*. *Fridays* was a knock-off of NBC's *Saturday Night Live* (and a pretty good one, too) that

---

172    https://www.vulture.com/2020/08/interview-elliot-easton-on-the-cars-and-ric-ocasek.html?ocid=uxbndlbing

included a pre-*Seinfeld* and *Curb Your Enthusiasm* Larry David among its cast members.

**"Touch and Go"** was the highlight of ***Panorama***, the Cars third album. Released as a single in the U.S., the song only got to #37 on the Billboard Hot 100, whereas ***Panorama*** went to #5. Even so, the album failed to sell nearly as well as the Cars' 1978 **debut album** or 1979's ***Candy-O***. The song **"Panorama"** was accompanied by a strange video that fall. But, then again, it was a strange time.

Ocasek and the Cars would right the ship in 1981 with the album and single "Shake it Up," but John wouldn't be around to see that.

BLONDIE

"The Tide Is High"

*Autoamerican*

In a 2006 interview Sean Lennon remembered his father's love for Blondie's cover of "**The Tide Is High**," a song that was originally recorded by the Paragons in Jamaica in 1967:

> "My father had an Old Wurlitzer (jukebox) in the game room of our house on Long Island. It was filled with 45s, mostly Elvis and the Everly Brothers. The one modern song I remember him listening to was "**The Tide Is High**," which he played constantly. When I hear that song I see my father, unshaven, his hair pulled back into a pony tail, dancing to and fro in a wore out pair of denim shorts, with me at his feet."[173]

"**The Tide Is High**" was first recorded by the Paragons in 1967, and was written by their lead singer, John Holt. Holt would go on to a very successful solo career before passing away in 2014. The song is a prime example of the Rocksteady era in Jamaican music, which lasted from about 1966 to 1968. Rocksteady descended from ska and gave birth to reggae. Blondie's gently swaying cover of "**The Tide is High**" utilized session musicians and doesn't stray too far from the original. The U.S. B-side of "**The Tide Is High**" was "**Suzy & Jeffrey**," a bouncy number in

---

173     Austin Scaggs, "Q &A: Sean Lennon," *Rolling Stone,* September 21, 2006, https://www.rollingstone.com/music/music-news/qa-sean-lennon-105993/

the style of Blondie's 1979 hit—and one of John favorites—"**Dreamin'**."

And 1980 was a great year for Blondie. In March "**Atomic**" (featuring Robert Fripp on guitar) from their *Eat to the Beat* album earned the band their third U.K. no. 1 song. "**Atomic**" is a very modern-sounding song[174], not dissimilar in style from "**Heart of Glass**." Then their song "**Call Me**" from the movie *American Gigolo* topped the U.S. Hot 100 chart for six weeks during April and May. Only one other song would duplicate that feat in 1980. That was Kenny Rogers' ballad "**Lady**" (written by the soon-to-be household name Lionel Ritchie), which had a six-week run at no. 1 during November and December before being replaced by John's "**(Just Like) Starting Over**" following John's death. As determined by *Billboard*, "**Call Me**" was the most popular song of 1980 in the U.S.

"**The Tide Is High**" was at no. 32 on Billboard's December 6 singles chart, up six places. It didn't make it to no. 1 until January 31, 1981, when it displaced John's own "**(Just Like) Starting Over**" atop the U.S. *Billboard* Hot 100. It's interesting that John was on to "**The Tide Is High**" immediately upon its release in the weeks before his death. A possible explanation is that the song topped the U.K. chart on November 15, shortly after its release. Another reason was the fact that, as we've seen, John was a big fan of Blondie. In his BBC interview two days before his death John said: "I saw Blondie when she was unknown on the cable TV[175]… thing they have here." That means John had been following

---

174    R.E.M. sound like they're channeling "**Atomic**" on their excellent 2001 song "All the Way to Reno."

175    Due to its tall buildings wreaking havoc with over-the-air television reception, Manhattan was one of the few places in the U.S. during the mid-1970s to be wired for cable TV. John had a Manhattan cable box in his bedroom. While attending a reception at the Copacabana club for director Elia Kazan and the premiere of the movie *The Last Tycoon* in September 1976, John was interviewed by the host of one of these shows, the notorious "Ugly George" Urban of *The Ugly George Hour*. This show often featured the host trying to convince random women to undress in front

Blondie since they first came on the New York scene in 1976 with an early '60s girl group sound and songs like "**X-Offender**."

In her 2019 memoir *Face It*[176] Debbie Harry reveals that mutual friend photographer Bob Gruen was making plans for her and partner/bandmate Chris Stein to meet John and Yoko. In addition, they had dropped off a copy of their new album *Autoamerican* for John at the Dakota, and had "Heard that John played it all the time." The meeting, planned to take place at the Dakota that December, never took place.

*Autoamerican* includes "**Rapture**," a groundbreaking song that was the first rap song that would to hit no. 1 in the U.S. in the spring of 1981. Note that in November 1980 John recorded a brief rap-like song idea entitled "**Pop Is the Name of the Game**" on his final demo tape. We'll never know if he was inspired by "**Rapture**," but it's theoretically possible. Unbeknownst to listeners in 1980, rap and hip-hop would go on to be the dominant pop music genre of the 1980s and '90s and beyond. Although it's hard to imagine John becoming a rapper, he was, at least, open to appreciating the new genre, something that you couldn't say about too many of his contemporaries at the time.

*Autoamerican* is a change of pace for Blondie, starting with the lead-off track "**Europa**," an orchestrated piece that sounds like it might be the soundtrack in search of a movie. Other experiments include an out of left-field version of the song "**Follow Me**" from Lerner & Loewe's Broadway hit *Camelot*. Although slagged by some critics at the time—*Rolling Stone* called it a "terrible album"—*Autoamerican* has aged well and doesn't sound dated forty years on.

---

of his camera. John is obviously familiar with the show as George quizzes him about sex and nudity. Brief as it is, this is one of only two interviews filmed with him during the "house husband" years. The Ugly George clip was on YouTube as of this writing. Debbie Harry later appeared on the show, also.

176   Debbie Harry, *Face It* (New York: Dey St., 2019)

Despite spawning two no. 1 singles, ***Autoamerican*** marked the beginning of the end of the first phase of Blondie's career. Their 1982 album, *The Hunter*, was a critical and commercial bust and the band soon went their separate ways. Incredibly, the reunited Blondie scored another U.K. no. 1 song (their sixth) two decades later with "Maria" in 1999.

CAPTAIN BEEFHEART & THE MAGIC BAND
"Hot Head" and "Ashtray Heart"
*Saturday Night Live* November 22, 1980

This *Saturday Night Live* episode was hosted by actor Malcolm McDowell, best known for his role as Alex in Stanley Kubrick's 1971 film *A Clockwork Orange*. Based on the 1962 Anthony Burgess novel of the same name, the film depicts a violent, dystopian future. Alex and his band of "Droogs" literally rape and pillage their way through the movie. At one point in the *SNL* show, McDowell does a skit dressed as Alex.

In early 1968 all four Beatles signed a letter to writer Terry Southern[177], who'd been tasked with adapting the book to the big screen, urging the casting of Mick Jagger in the role of Alex, instead of David Hemmings of *Blow Up* fame. This was before Kubrick, with whom Southern had collaborated on the screenplay to *Dr. Strangelove*, took over the film. Jagger, who at one time owned the film rights to *A Clockwork Orange*, thought the Beatles would provide the soundtrack if he got the role of Alex.

This was the second episode of *SNL's* troubled sixth season, during which an entirely new cast premiered to replace what remained of the original "Not Ready for Prime Time Players." This occurred along with the departure (temporarily, as it turned out) of producer Lorne Michaels and the installation of a new producer, Jean Doumanian. *SNL* aficionados rate this show as possibly the worst episode of the show's over 40-year

---

177    Ringo would star in the 1968 movie *Candy*, the film of the 1958 novel co-authored by Southern, and *1969's The Magic Christian*, based on Southern's 1959 comic novel. The latter film featured Badfinger's hit version of "**Come and Get It**," which was written and produced by Paul McCartney.

run. In his *RKO* interview of December 8, John and Yoko spoke of how they enjoyed a send-up of themselves on this episode's "Weekend Update" segment. "John and Yoko" (McDowell and Denny Dillion) were interviewed by Charles Rocket who asks about their new album. "It's mostly love songs and baking tips," replies "John."

Captain Beefheart (aka Don Van Vliet) & The Magic Band performed "**Hot Head**" just before the Weekend Update segment. Later in the show they do "**Ashtray Heart**," another song from their then current album, ***Doc at the Radar Station***. "**Ashtray Heart**" deals with Beefheart's feelings about young New Wave musicians whom he felt had appropriated his sound without crediting him. With a singing voice that channeled Howlin' Wolf and jittery "songs,"—not dissimilar to Yoko's Plastic Ono Band offerings—Beefheart was surely one of rock's most idiosyncratic characters. Although hardly a commercial success, ***Doc at the Radar Station*** is considered by Beefheart fans to be one of his better albums, and it placed at no. 6 in the *Village Voice's* prestigious "Pazz and Jop" poll of critics' favorite albums of 1980. Easy listening it ain't.

Some claimed that Beefheart was a clairvoyant, that he would know the telephone was going to ring before it rang, or know that a person had entered a building without being able to see them. Guitarist Gary Lucas later related a strange story about the night of December 8, when Beefheart—still in New York staying at Lucas's apartment—was giving interviews to music journalists:

> "In the middle of the interview, at eight or nine o'clock as I
> remember, Don said 'Wait a minute, man, did you hear that?'
> He put his hand over his ear but we didn't hear anything. He
> said 'Something really heavy just went down. I can't tell you
> what it is exactly, but you will read about it on the front page

of the newspapers tomorrow. We said, 'Well, what?' and he said 'I dunno.' (Upon hearing the news of the shooting later that night) I just couldn't believe it. It really seemed like Don predicted this. So I told him and he just looked at me and went 'See? Didn't I tell you?' That was really eerie."[178]

Beefheart would release only one more album, 1982's *Ice Cream for Crow*, before retiring from the music business to become a painter. He died at the age of sixty-nine in December 2010 having spent the last decades of his life out of the public eye. His 1967 album **Safe as Milk** is an outstanding album and the best introduction to Beefheart's music for the uninitiated. In 1967 John was photographed at his Weybridge home with a **Safe as Milk** promo sticker on his wall. This indicates that he owned the **Safe as Milk** album because the stickers came with the original U.S. pressing of the Buddah Records album.

John had worked with Beefheart's friend and sometime collaborator Frank Zappa when they jammed at the Fillmore East in New York in June of 1971. Some of those recordings turned up on John and Yoko's **Some Time in New York City** album the following year. John owned a copy of Zappa and the Mothers of Invention's 1968 album **Cruising with Ruben and the Jets**, their twisted homage to the Doo-wop music of the 1950s. (You've never heard **Jelly Roll Gum Drop** or **Cheap Thrills**? Clearly, your life is incomplete!)

In introducing the "John and Yoko" skit, Rocket makes reference to the previous week's show when he "almost" got an interview with John and Yoko. In that show from November 15, Rocket does a field segment in which he goes to the Dakota in search of the inside story on the

---

178   "Captain Beefheart's Eerie Premonition of John Lennon's Death," Dangerous Minds, https://dangerousminds.net/comments/captain_beefhearts_eerie_premonition_of_john_lennon

new John and Yoko album, which was about to be released on Monday, November 17th. Rocket introduces the segment with the Dakota behind him. He proceeds to speak to an old lady on a nearby park bench who states "I know Lennon is in that building because all the youngsters gather there to get an autograph. ... Why do they allow them to gather there?" Good question.

Next, we see a few scattered young people hanging out near the entrance to the Dakota. Rocket asked a few questions of the doorman, who stands only a few feet away from where John will be slain in less than a month. Needless to say, a bit that was supposed to make people laugh is both appalling and horrifying in retrospect. While John and Yoko's residence was hardly a secret (John and Yoko stand beside the building on the corner of W. 72nd St. and Central Park West on the back cover of **Double Fantasy**), and there was no apparent causal relationship between this *SNL* broadcast and John's assassination three weeks later, you wonder what SNL producers were thinking.

The fact that John and Yoko were subjects of *SNL* segments during two consecutive weeks is testament to the perceived public interest in John's comeback.

## LEO SAYER

"More Than I Can Say"

**"More Than I Can Say"** was the no. 2 song in the U.S. the week that John died. It was being kept out of the top spot by Kenny Rogers' **"Lady,"** which had been no. 1 since November 15. Written by Lionel Ritchie, who would become one the most successful artists of the '80s upon leaving the Commodores to go solo, **"Lady"** would stay atop the charts until December 27, when it was dislodged but John's **"(Just Like) Starting Over."**

John had been aware of **"More Than I Can Say"** for years.

This song was originally recorded by the Crickets in 1960, one year after Buddy Holly's death. Bobby Vee had a minor hit with it in the U.S. the following year, but his version rose to no. 4 in the U.K. charts and that was how Sayer—and John—became aware of the song. **"More Than I Can Say"** was written by drummer Jerry Allison and new Cricket, singer/guitarist Sonny Curtis. Curtis also composed the Bobby Fuller Four classic **"I Fought the Law,"** the Everly Brothers 1960 hit **"Walk Right Back,"** and the Mary Tyler Moore show theme **"Love Is All Around."** The Clash's recording of **"I Fought the Law"** was released as the band's single in the U.S. in mid-1979 and helped introduce the band to American audiences.

The Beatles recorded the post-Holly Crickets song **"Don't Ever Change"** (a Goffin-King number that) for the BBC on August 1, 1963[179],

---

179   In a rare Paul and George duet, no less.

and they reportedly played "**More Than I Can Say**" in concert in 1961 and 1962, although no recording is known to exist.

Sayer had several hits while John was on hiatus including "**Long Tall Glasses**" in 1975, and "**You Make Me Feel Like Dancin'**" and "**When I Need You**," both of which topped the U.S. *Billboard* singles chart in 1977. Sayer also saw success as a songwriter when Three Dog Night had a hit with his song "**The Show Must Go On**" in 1974. Likewise, Cliff Richard was still on the chart in late 1980 with Sayer's song "**Suddenly**." "**More Than I Can Say**" was something of a comeback for Sayer, but also marked the last time he would trouble the U.S. Top Ten.

ELVIS COSTELLO

"(What's So Funny 'Bout) Peace, Love and Understanding"

A standout track on Costello's excellent third album, *Armed Forces*, this song had been written in 1974 by the album's producer, Nick Lowe. Lowe recorded it with his band at the time, the beloved, if underachieving British pub-rock outfit Brinsley Schwarz. Their version was the first song on *The New Favourites of... Brinsley Schwarz*, an album produced by another Lennon favorite, Dave Edmunds. Originally envisioned by Lowe as a sort of ironic comment on hippie philosophy, Costello gave it an angry, urgent, and pleading spin. Costello's recording became the definitive version of the song, and the *only* one with which most listeners are familiar. Thus **"(What's So Funny 'Bout) Peace, Love and Understanding"**—no doubt aided by the somewhat less than ideal state of the world—has shed its irony and gone on to become a modern classic.

In his interview with Jonathon Cott, John cited **"(What's So Funny 'Bout) Peace, Love and Understanding"** in explaining how he now thought about life:

> "I'm older now. I see the world through different eyes now. But I still believe in peace, love and understanding as Elvis Costello said. What's so fucking funny about peace, love and understanding? It's fashionable to be a go-getter and slash thy

neighbor with a cross, but we're not ones to follow the fashion."[180].

In the late 1980s Costello formed a brief, but successful writing partnership with Paul McCartney. The press liked to point out that Costello had supposedly stepped into the Lennon role of supplying the acid to McCartney's treacle. Big shoes to fill, to say the least! The partnership did manage to turn out some of McCartney's best songs in years including "Veronica," "Just Like Candy," and "My Brave Face." Many of their unreleased demos finally saw the light of day via the 2017 deluxe edition of McCartney's 1989 album *Flowers in the Dirt*.

Reflecting on the life of "**(What's So Funny 'Bout) Peace Love and Understanding**," the song he wrote long ago, Nick Lowe recently stated:

"That song started out as a joke. But I always suspected there was something more in it."[181]

Funny how where we are standing affects how we experience art, isn't it?

---

180    Jonathan Cott, *Days That I'll Remember*

181    Adrian Deevoy, "Whitney Houston Made Me a Million…" *The Daily Mail*, May 18, 2010

DAVE EDMUNDS
"Crawling from the Wreckage"


This was one of the last songs that John ever sang.[182] With the tape still rolling following the end of his RKO interview on the afternoon of the 8th, the RKO interviewers told John they were going to do an event with Rockpile, the band that included Edmunds and Nick Lowe. While John didn't immediately pick up on the name Rockpile, John immediately recognized Edmunds' and Lowe's names when interviewer mentioned them saying: "Oh I love Dave Edmunds. I love their stuff...**Crawling from the...**" John even sang a line from "**Crawling from the Wreckage**," a song **from** Edmunds' 1979 album *Repeat When Necessary*. John went on to say that Edmunds' 1970 cover of Smiley Lewis's Dave Bartholomew-penned "**I Hear You Knockin'**" was a favorite of his. John had extolled Edmunds' version way back in 1970 when he called it a "great one," explaining that "I always liked simple rock" in his lengthy *Rolling Stone* interview.

Nick Lowe and Dave Edmunds had been working together off and on since Edmunds produced Brinsley Schwartz's *The New Favourites of... Brinsley Schwarz*, which, as we've seen, contained the original recording of "**(What's So Funny 'Bout) Peace, Love, and Understanding.**" Rockpile coalesced in 1977 with guitarist Billy Bremner and drummer Terry Williams joining Lowe and Edmunds.

---

182    RKO's Dave Sholin later reported that John was singing Little Richard and Jerry Lee Lewis songs after the interview as they rode in the car to the Record Plant. See: Sharp, p. 229.

There were three de facto Rockpile albums before the group released the **Seconds of Pleasure** album under the Rockpile moniker in 1980. This explains why John didn't quite recognize the name Rockpile even though he was familiar with the work of both Lowe and Edmunds. After playing on Lowe's 1978 track "**Heart of the City**," the group backed Edmunds on his 1978 album **Tracks on Wax 4**. In 1978 they released Edmunds' **Repeat When Necessary** – which contains a cover of Elvis Costello's "**Girls Talk**" - and Lowe's **Labour of Lust**, which featured the top 20 U.S. hit "**Cruel to be Kind**."

"**Cruel to be Kind**" was co-written by Lowe and ex- Brinsley Schwarz band mate Ian Gomm. Gomm had a top 20 U.S. hit that of his own in the summer of 1979 with his wistful song **Hold On**.

Rockpile were among the acts that played at the *Concerts for the People of Kampuchea* at London's Hammersmith Odeon in December 1979. Amid media hype about a possible Beatles reunion at the show, Rockpile opened for Paul McCartney and Wings on the night of December 29 playing "**Crawling from the Wreckage**" and Elvis's" **Little Sister**" with guest vocalist Robert Plant. Although no one knew it at the time, this was to be the last ever Wings show.

Released in October 1980, **Seconds of Pleasure** contained the song "**Teacher Teacher**," which received strong FM airplay including on New York's WNEW-FM, where it's likely that John heard it.

"**Crawling from the Wreckage**" was written by Graham Parker. In terms of songwriting Parker had the talent to rival Costello and Springsteen, but he struggled to find commercial success. Parker's best album was 1979's **Squeezing Out Sparks** which was produced by Jack Nitzsche. It was praised as one of the best albums of the year in numerous publications and as the 1979 album of the year in the *Village Voice*'s Pazz & Jop critics poll, so it was likely on John's radar.

Costello, Lowe, Edmunds, Parker along with Chris Difford and Glenn Tilbrook of Squeeze – who's **Pulling Mussels (from the Shell)** was often played on New York radio during the summer of 1980 - were all talented songwriters playing a new wave version of the "simple rock" that John had always favored. All favored concise three-minute songs with sharp, sometimes caustic, lyrics. In this sense, John was something of a spiritual forefather to these artists and to New Wave/punk in general.

Parker covered John's song **"Bad to Me"** on the 2011 album *Lost Songs of Lennon and McCartney*. He got some much-deserved love when director Judd Apatow cast him and his reunited band The Rumour in the 2012 movie *This Is 40*.

While Parker may not have achieved the level of success many of his fans thought he deserved, knowing that John Lennon liked and sang your song has got to be gratifying.

*Double Fantasy* producer Jack Douglas went on to produce Parker's 1982 album *Another Grey Area*.

Dave Edmunds went on to produce George Harrison's excellent 1984 cover of Bob Dylan's obscure song "I Don't Want to Do It," which ended up on the Edmunds-produced *Porky's Revenge* soundtrack.

## THE VAPORS
"Turning Japanese"

A catchy new wave novelty that at times mimics traditional Japanese music (or westerners' idea of it), **"Turning Japanese"** received extensive airplay on U.S. radio in the autumn of 1980. The song got to no. 36 on the U.S. *Billboard* singles chart. It was an even bigger hit in the Vapors' native U.K., where it went to no. 3 earlier in the year. Given the fact that John was part of an Anglo-Japanese family, one can assume he would have had "**Turning Japanese**" on his radar.

The song is referenced (along with a quote from its lyrics) in an article[183] devoted to Yoko, not John, that appeared just days before John's death in the local New York City paper *The Soho Weekly News.* "**Turning Japanese**" is mentioned because patrons at the city's ultra-hip Peppermint Lounge club were dancing to it prior to the deejay spinning Yoko's ***Double Fantasy*** track "**Kiss Kiss Kiss**," which was arguably her strongest contribution to the album. John was so excited that Yoko was receiving recognition for her own work—in a publication widely read in New York art world—that he had an aide purchase many extra copies of the *Soho News* issue with Yoko on the cover. Moreover, he decided that Yoko needed to put out a track specifically aimed at the dance clubs like the ones playing "**Kiss, Kiss, Kiss.**"

Author Peter Ochiogrosso had spent hours interviewing Yoko for the article, which focused on her music and art. Yoko appeared on the cover

---

183   Peter Occhiogrosso, "Yoko Ono: Here's the Rest of Me" *The Soho News,* December 3, 1980.

next to a headline that read "Yoko Only," a headline that would soon take on an eerie aspect with John's death.

The fact that an influential deejay was playing the song was cited by Occhiogrosso in his article as evidence that "**Kiss Kiss Kiss**" was on its way to becoming a dance club hit. This was a prescient observation because several of Yoko's songs have indeed topped the dance charts during the subsequent decades. It turns out John was right when he told Yoko that "**Walking on Thin Ice**" would would be her first no. 1 record. Legendary New York deejay Larry Levan was among those who played "**Walking on Thin Ice**" in clubs when it was released in January 1981.

It's interesting to note that both the Vapors' and Yoko's songs apparently reference orgasms (male and female respectively). "**Turning Japanese was** widely assumed to be about guys pleasuring themselves (although the composer, Vapors lead singer and guitarist David Fenton denied this, saying it was actually referring to how his relationship troubles were driving him crazy) and the end of "**Kiss Kiss Kiss**" features Yoko vocalizing the sounds of a woman climaxing. As such, "**Kiss Kiss Kiss**" is a linear descendant of Jane Birkin and Serge Gainsbourg's 1969 hit "**Je t'aime…Moi Non Plus**" and Donna Summer's debut disco smash from 1975, "**Love to Love You Baby**."

By the time the "Yoko Only" issue hit newsstands on Wednesday, December 3, John, Yoko, and Jack Douglas were already back at the Record Plant (chosen because Douglas was working on an album for another artist there) finishing "**Walking on Thin Ice**." In a tip of the hat to the article that inspired the effort, the prospective title of the proposed EP was "Yoko Only."

Occhiogrosso was invited to attend the Thursday night "**Walking on Thin Ice**" recording session. There John confirmed to him that the reason they were there finishing "**Walking on Thin Ice**" was because the

Peppermint Lounge deejay had played "**Kiss Kiss Kiss**" as reported in the *Soho News* story. Yoko was recording vocal overdubs that night and John would occasionally offer a suggestion to her or Douglas. The writer recalled meeting John at the studio:

> "That night left me with an overwhelming impression. Not only was this guy not the burn-out Borgia that everyone, myself included, made him out to be, but he was a friendlier and funnier guy than most of the people I know...John was incredibly proud that Yoko was finally having her day. The *Soho* cover story, her sudden recognition in the trendy world of rock dance spots and her prospects for future glory were turning him on. "[184]

The Vapors hailed from Guildford, Surrey, and were proteges of The Jam, having been "discovered" by Jam bassist Bruce Foxton. The Vapors' career evaporated in 1981 after their second album tanked. "**Turning Japanese**" lives on, however, regularly turning up in movies and television commercials.

---

[184]  Peter Occhiogrossso, "John Lennon: A Day in the Light," *The Soho News,* December 10, 1980

SANFORD CLARK
"The Fool"

John told writer Jonathan Cott during their Friday night interview that his guitar playing on Yoko's "**Walking on Thin Ice**" was inspired by Clark's 1956 hit "**The Fool**." It might seem counterintuitive to insert a guitar lick from a record that was almost a quarter century old onto what was the most adventurous recording John had done in years, but that's what geniuses do. John's new work throughout 1980 was consistently inspired by the rock and roll artists that turned him on to the music when he was a teenager. On "**Walking on Thin Ice**," he lets loose with some of his most creative guitar playing in years. He later told Yoko that his guitar solo on "**Walking on Thin Ice**" was the best thing he'd ever played. You have to listen closely to hear the echoes of "**The Fool**" on the track, but they are there.

Clark is something of a mysterious figure. Despite the fact that "**The Fool**" rose to no. 6 (it also went into the top 20 on both the country and R&B charts) during rock and roll's breakthrough year of 1956, Clark seemed strangely disinterested in promoting the song. Clark later had a minor hit with his 1959 cowboy saga "**Son of a Gun**." (In his autobiography, *Life*, Keith Richards wrote that "**Son of a Gun**" was the first song he ever performed onstage.) By 1960 Clark had joined the Air Force. He later became a croupier and only sang and recorded on the side.

"**The Fool**" was co-written by Lee Hazlewood and his wife, Naomi Ford. Guitarist Al Casey (he later of L.A. "Wrecking Crew" fame) heard

JOHN LENNON : 1980 PLAYLIST

Clark perform and introduced him to Hazlewood. They recorded "**The Fool**" in Phoenix, Arizona, at Audio Recording Studios. This is the same studio where guitarist Duane Eddy would soon record his string of hits. Working with Hazlewood and Casey, Eddy's hits included "**Rebel Rouser**," "**Shazam**," "**Peter Gunn**," "**Forty Miles of Bad Road**," "**Moanin' 'N Twistin'**," "**Three 30 Blues**," "**Because They're Young**,"[185] and in 1962 "**(Dance with the) Guitar Man**." Both Paul McCartney and George Harrison contributed to Eddy's 1987 album *Duane Eddy*.

Of course, Hazlewood went on to chart his own circuitous musical career that included writing and producing "**These Boots Were Made for Walking**" for Nancy Sinatra, who once described Lee as "a combination of Henry Higgins and Sigmund Freud." Lee also duetted with Nancy on hit songs like "**Jackson**," "**Some Velvet Morning**," and "**Sand**." (You've really got to listen to "**Sand**.") Hazlewood also co-produced Nancy's 1967 duet with her father, Frank, "**Something Stupid**," a no. 1 from the "Summer of Love" that features Casey on guitar.

Elvis Presley covered "The Fool," a faithful version released on his 1971 album *Elvis Country*.

---

185    Later to inspire the guitar riff in Bruce Springsteen's "**Born to Run**."

YOKO ONO
"Walking on Thin Ice"


Asked about writing "**Walking on Thin Ice**" in 2000, Yoko stated:

"It just came to me and I just wrote it. It was like (snaps fingers)—it was like that. It was channeling maybe. It might have been kind of—a premonition?"[186]

John devoted the last days of his life to this song. Yoko recorded her spoken poem section – inspired by a memory of the vastness of Lake Michigan which she noted during a visit to Chicago - when the song was being completed in the days before John's death.

In her note on the sleeve of the 45 of "**Walking on Thin Ice**," Yoko recalled that both she and John were "haunted" by the song the weekend before he died. She recalled that she found John listening to the song early in the morning, just as he had been the previous night. Like "**Help Me to Help Myself**" and "**Borrowed Time**," the song seems to refer to the possibility of impending tragedy. It's also a modern, sophisticated dance track, quite unlike anything else that Yoko or John had recorded before.

When writer Jonathan Cott inquired as to why he and Yoko were at the Record Plant on Friday night December 5, replied that "We did come in here to make a string of songs that might go to the rock and

---

186   Conversation with Jody Denberg recorded September 7, 2000, in New York City.

disco clubs."[187]

At the Record Plant on December 8, John said to label boss David Geffen: "Wait 'til you hear Yoko's record. It's a smash! It's better than *anything* we did on **Double Fantasy**." When Yoko expressed skepticism at that, John replied "It is. It's better that anything the B-52s[188] ever did. And we want you to put it out before Christmas."[189] Despite John's enthusiasm, Geffen suggested that waiting until the new year was a more prudent course. After all, Christmas was only a little over two weeks away. Geffen also informed John and Yoko that **Double Fantasy** had gone gold in the U.S. was set to go to no. 1 on the U.K. charts, an achievement that had to be especially heartening to John, who had always kept an eye on the U.K. scene and was disappointed when earlier albums were not well received in his homeland.

According to some sources,[190] "**Walking on Thin Ice**" was including on a late August list attempting to establish a running order on the tracks that would constitute **Double Fantasy**. On this list it was slated to lead off the second side of the album. Although Jack Douglas would describe the "**Walking on Thin Ice**" track taped for **Double Fantasy** as a "loop," this would indicate it has been developed enough—or was going to be—to merit being shortlisted for the album. Earl Slick later recalled playing on "**Walking on Thin Ice**" during the **Double Fantasy** sessions, and he wasn't present during the December sessions. Slick recently called the track "One of my top recorded moments. ...

---

187   Cott

188   The B-52s second album, **Wild Planet**, had been released at the end of August and included the songs "**Party Out of Bounds**," "**Give Me Back My Man**," and "**Private Idaho**." It was at no. 57 on the *Billboard* album chart as John spoke.

189   *Rolling Stone,* January 22, 1981.

190   Madinger and Raille

John and I did some really cool stuff on that record."[191]

Douglas later stated that both he and John were playing guitar during the mixing process. Recalling the last night in the studio, Douglas recalled: "We just listened to (**"Walking on Thin Ice"**) over and over. We were so happy with it."[192]

**"Walking on Thin Ice"** will forever stand as the last piece of art created by one of the twentieth century's greatest artists. John held a tape of **"Walking on Thin Ice"** in his hand when he fell later that night.

191   Jeff Slate, "Earl Slick: My 12 greatest recordings of all time," Music Radar, February 26, 2013, https://www.musicradar.com/news/guitars/earl-slick-my-12-greatest-recordings-of-all-time-571523

192   Kurt Loder, "John Lennon: The Last Session," *Rolling Stone,* January 22, 1981.

## DOMINIC BEHAN
"Liverpool Lou"

During a 2007 appearance on the BBC's *Desert Island Discs* program Yoko said that after leaving the Record Plant on the night of December 8 John wanted to return home to see Sean before he went to sleep, rather than going to dinner. She said she chose "**Liverpool Lou**" as one of her desert island songs because she "When Sean was born, he would just sing the song to him until he goes to sleep. Almost every night." She said John once described "**Liverpool Lou**" as "a beautiful song."

Behan was the brother of hard partying Irish writer Brendan Behan, the author of *Borstal Boy*. Dominic wrote the song "**The Patriot Game**" which was soon purloined by Bob Dylan for his song "**With God on Our Side**". Dominic did little to hide his resentment of Dylan over this for the rest of his life.

Behan released his version of "**Liverpool Lou**" in 1964. It is more of a lover's lament than a lullaby. "**Liverpool Lou**" has been recorded many times through the years, notably by the Dubliners and Scaffold, who had an unlikely top 10 UK hit with the song in 1974. Scaffold recorded their version at the suggestion of one Paul McCartney, whose brother Mike (McGear) was a member of Scaffold. Paul produced and arranged Scaffold's recording of "**Liverpool Lou**," and he also plays bass and likely contributed backing vocals.

Prior to recording "**Liverpool Lou**," Paul, Linda and members of Wings assisted Mike with the recording of his debut solo album, *McGear*.

Since he co-wrote the songs and plays and sings on every track, this is something of a lost Paul McCartney album. *McGear* captures Wings in their heyday during the downtime following the recording of ***Band on the Run***. One song, "**Rainbow Lady**," is as good or better than much of Paul's own work at the time.

Perhaps John would have sung "**Liverpool Lou**" to Sean that Monday night. If only he'd made it home.

Made in the USA
Coppell, TX
18 December 2020